Praise for *Gifts of the Dark Wood*

"Many of us have known Eric Elnes as a brilliant theologian, daring communicator, and creative genius. But in *Gifts of the Dark Wood*, we get to know Eric as a sensitive pastor and wise spiritual director or guide. In his care through these pages, readers will be touched by insight, humility, inspiration, consolation, and profound joy, and they will find themselves discovering rich treasures in most unexpected places—in their failures, their darkness, their disappointment." —**Brian D. McLaren**, author and activist, brianmclaren.net

"Eric Elnes is one of post-liberal Christianity's most thoughtful, effective, and influential leaders. An informed and teaching pastor to both his local congregation and to his communion-at-large, he ministers also to the thousands from around the world who worship with him each week in the cyber-church, Darkwood Brew." —**Phyllis Tickle**, author of *Emergence Christianity*

"As both a friend of Eric's work and of the man, let me say that *Gifts of the Dark Wood* is his finest achievement. Eric writes with the fierce honesty of a mystic, the soul of a true priest—one who truly ministers to others—and the pen of a prophet. This is a road map giving us a path for following the Spirit." —**Frank Schaeffer**, author of *Why I Am an Atheist Who Believes in God*

" 'In a dark time, the eye begins to see,' wrote the American poet Theodore Roethke. This paradox is at the heart of Eric Elnes's deeply felt book. Drawing on examples from his own life, from his ministry, and from the scriptures, he shows how bewilderment may yield insight and how, by getting lost, we may find our way. Whether the dark time that concerns you is personal, due to private suffering, or public, due to widely shared afflictions such as war and social injustice and environmental devastation, you will find wise guidance in these pages." —**Scott Russell Sanders**, author of *Earth Works: Selected Essays*

GIFTS
OF THE
DARK
WOOD

**SEVEN BLESSINGS FOR
SOULFUL SKEPTICS
(AND OTHER WANDERERS)**

ERIC ELNES

ABINGDON PRESS | NASHVILLE

GIFTS OF THE DARK WOOD
SEVEN BLESSINGS FOR SOULFUL SKEPTICS (AND OTHER WANDERERS)

Copyright © 2015 by Eric Elnes

Library of Congress Cataloging-in-Publication Data

ISBN 978-1-4267-9413-1

Elnes, Eric.
  Gifts of the dark wood : seven blessings for soulful skeptics (and other wanderers) / Eric Elnes.
     pages cm
  Includes bibliographical references.
  ISBN 978-1-4267-9413-1 (binding: soft back)   1. Spiritual life—Christianity.   I. Title.
  BV4501.3.E4585 2015
  248—dc23

                                                                      2015004788

15 16 17 18 19 20 21 22 23 24—10 9 8 7 6 5 4 3 2 1
MANUFACTURED IN THE UNITED STATES OF AMERICA

This book is dedicated to Bob and Gretchen Ravenscroft and to the memory of my father, Conrad Elnes.

CONTENTS

ACKNOWLEDGMENTS

AMERICAN POET AND ESSAYIST Walt Whitman once observed that, "a leaf of grass is no less than the journey-work of the stars." As I turn through the leaves of this book, I find myself in awe over how many brilliant "stars" have contributed significant insight, guidance, and affirmation over the course of various drafts of this humble work. Among them are authors, including David James Duncan, Scott Russell Sanders, Phyllis Tickle, Frank Schaeffer, and Lauren Winner. Others include my literary agent, Kathryn Helmers, as well as many friends including Patti Tu, Chris Alexander, Cary Sharkey, Cyndi Kugler, Leslie Murrell, Deb McCollister, Margaret McGrath, Bob and Gretchen Ravenscroft, Donna and Paul Knutson, Dove DoVale, and Scott and Anna Griessel. My family played an enormous role as well with respect to both content and moral support—especially my wife, Melanie; her sister, Corrie Gant; my daughters, Arianna and Maren; and my parents, Phyllis and Conrad. My hope is that these pages reflect at least a portion of your brilliance.

Most of all, I am grateful to the members and friends of Countryside Community Church (UCC) in Omaha, Nebraska, two hundred of whom read the first draft of this book and contributed meaningful feedback. Another fifty of these helped create an engaging video series, "Gifts of the Dark Wood," produced by Darkwood Brew (www.darkwoodbrew.org) to accompany this book. Guests appearing on this series engaged with this book from their own perspective, adding depth, insight, and frequent humor. These include Parker Palmer, Diana Butler-Bass, Brian McLaren, Lillian Daniel, Frank Schaeffer, Melvin Bray, Chuck Marohnic, and *Semisonic*'s drummer, Jacob Slichter. All of you inspire and amaze me.

Finally, significant portions of this book were written while on various writing retreats. I am grateful to Dr. David and Judy Magill, who graciously allowed me full use of their beautiful Sedona, Arizona, home, as well as to the good folks at Spirit of the Desert Retreat Center in Carefree, Arizona. The "stars" at Arcosanti, an environmentally sustainable community in Mayer, Arizona, are particularly dear to my heart. Portions of this book and two others have been written while enjoying their hospitality, vision, and creative spirit at their high desert oasis.

INTRODUCTION

A PLACE
IN THIS WORLD

EASEDALE TARN. CRESTING THE BROW of a ridge overlooking a small mountain lake in the north of England, most of my hiking companions stopped for a brief lunch before moving on to the next ridge. After the lunch break, I swallowed my pride and decided to stay behind with a couple of others. It was against my nature, but my knees, which hadn't quite been the same since walking across the United States in 2006, were still protesting the arduous ups and downs of the preceding day's hike.

Finishing lunch on top of a sun-warmed boulder a few yards up from shore, I found the waters of the lake too tempting to be left alone. Their depths seemed to be held in place by two knobby hands cupped and held tightly together, as a wanderer in the Lake District might cup her hands before dipping them to drink from a stream.

The mountain's granite peaks looked down over the lake in front of us like guards standing watch on a castle wall. The grassy slopes coddling us from behind held the wind at bay, allowing the lake to rest in perfect stillness, beckoning the sky to come down and lay upon it.

"The lake will be cold!" one of my companions warned. Staying comfortable was not my concern. Interloper though I was, the perfection before me seemed to invite company.

Stripping down as far as modesty would allow, I gingerly stepped forward, trying neither to cut my feet on the sharp granite at the edge of the lake, nor to slip on the smooth, slimy rocks in the shallows. I was feeling particularly awkward. My slightly protruding belly had gained another three inches in the years since the 2006 walk and my stumbling around caused certain parts of me to jiggle more than others. At the first opportunity, I lurched forward into the water hoping to bury my paunch before anyone noticed.

"How's the water?" called the mothering companion.

"Not bad, actually," I answered a bit too hastily.

As the greater part of the group made its way up the ridge above the lake, I inched out toward the lake's center, imagining how poor my strokes must appear to onlookers. My butterfly was an inchworm. My crawl, a stumble.

Soon, my skin started to resemble a plucked turkey against the increasing chill of the water. "Guess I spoke too soon," I told myself as my remaining companions prepared themselves for a swim.

Seeking warmth and tired of my awkwardness in the water, I stopped, treaded momentarily, then tilted my head back and thrust my chest forward until the length of my body rose to meet the lake's sun-drenched surface.

"Ah, that extra bit of belly is good for something," I told myself as I effortlessly floated without increasing or deepening my breathing in any way. I felt like one of the drifting clouds reflected on the lake's surface.

As the late afternoon sun bathed and dried my face, neck, chest, and toes, some imperceptible breeze slowly turned me until my feet pointed like a compass straight toward the grassy slopes where I'd eaten lunch. My gaze shifted from the wispy clouds and surrounding blueness above to the tan boulders nestled in the green grass. For a moment, my protruding toes seemed to merge perfectly with the boulders. Body thus united with mountain, water, and sky, I could almost hear a quiet voice whisper, *You have a place in this world; a place where everything comes together in your body and you disappear into a seamless whole. Get over your clumsiness, and your fat little belly, and inhabit this world with your fullest self.*

A few minutes later, the breeze picked up, breaking both the surface of the water and my concentration. Feeling the water's chill once again, I made my way toward shore. Rising cautiously above the surface, aware again of my belly, and then nearly slipping on the green rocks beneath, I suddenly lost hold of the peace I had grasped just moments earlier. But then a quiet certainty smoothed itself over me. It seemed to whisper, *The peace you just let go of is not ready to let go of you.* I took another step forward, reminded that I not only have a place in this world but also that the world has a place in me.

WHERE WE FIND OURSELVES

In the middle of the road of my life I awoke in a Dark Wood
where the true way was wholly lost.
—Dante Alighieri

YOU HAVE A PLACE IN THIS WORLD. It is a place where awkwardness dissolves and you are most fully alive, therefore most fully human. You know this place very well, though you may feel far from it. Take a deep breath and hold it briefly. Exhale slowly. You *know* this place. You may not always know how to get to it, but you recognize it every time.

Likely you first sensed its existence in early childhood. Over the subsequent course of your life, you may have stumbled into—and out of—this place of aliveness many times, especially during periods of significant upheaval or transition. These were brief moments of awakening when something way down inside suddenly leapt to attention and cried, "Home!" Yet much of the time, you may feel far from home. *You are closer than you realize.* Much of the time you may feel more like Pinocchio, woodenly meandering through life, hoping to be alive one day. *That day could be today.*

This book is about finding your place in this world at the very point where you feel furthest from it. It's about recognizing the fierce beauty and astonishing blessing that exists within experiences that most of us fear but none of us can avoid. Ultimately this book is about seeing life through new eyes, recognizing that experiences of failure, emptiness, and uncertainty are as critical for finding our way through life as they are unavoidable. These experiences frequently offer clues, in fact, to what the ancients would name our "calling" or "path in life." A number of these clues come through experiences of spiritual awakening that present themselves not in the absence of struggle, but deep in the heart of it.

Years ago, I made a list of my proudest achievements in life. Looking over the list, I was struck by the realization that nearly everything on my list was directly or indirectly the result of some failure, loss, or disappointment that forced me to look at my situation differently and produced a creative result. What I experienced as loss in hindsight proved to be the loss of an old way of life that was in the process of giving way to something new. Many times when my expectations had been disappointed and I felt like God was furthest from me, God had actually drawn closest but had approached from a direction I wasn't expecting. What I experienced as emptiness often was an emptying of old patterns of behavior or thought that prepared me to see that the direction I was heading was no longer working. A new direction was revealed that would yield more promising results. My frequent experiences of uncertainty were what developed a deeper sense of trust that emboldened me to follow a call into uncharted territory.

In light of these realizations, I began to view not only my life story but also the lives of my great childhood heroes differently—many of them were from the Bible. Others included heroes like Abraham Lincoln, George Washington Carver, Dorothy Day, and Martin Luther King, Jr. To be sure, these heroes could produce a lengthy list of accomplishments. Yet their list of failures and "dark nights of the soul" was every bit as long. Their stories reminded me that I wasn't alone in my struggles. They showed that living a vital, even heroic, life is not about moving from temporary failure to lasting success, but allowing your next struggle to become your next source of revelation, thereby your next opportunity.

In light of these realizations, the Jewish and Christian Scriptures took on an added dimension in which their stories of faith and doubt gained surprising new relevancy for my life. For instance, one of my other great childhood heroes was the apostle Peter. There is a curious story concerning Peter in the Gospels where Jesus' disciples spot Jesus late one night walking upon the Sea of Galilee in the middle of a storm. Terrified, they think he's a ghost. "Don't be afraid," Jesus assures them, "It's really me." Then one of them named Simon (later renamed Peter), calls out, "Lord, if it's you, then command me to come out on the water." Jesus does so and Simon boldly steps out of the boat. Much to everyone's surprise, Simon actually walks on top of the water, at least for a few steps according to the story. When it dawns on him exactly where he is and what he is doing, Simon sinks like a rock, reaching desperately for Jesus crying, "Save me!" Jesus grasps Simon's hand and draws him back to the boat.

Shortly thereafter, surrounded by the disciples, Jesus announces that he has a new name for Simon. He changes Simon's name to Peter, which means "rock." I can imagine the cackling of the disciples: "Ha! Peter you *sank* like a rock! The name fits you perfectly. When people think they can become powerful and self-righteous by following Jesus, we'll just tell them to go talk to 'The Rock.' You'll disabuse them of their fantasies!"

In the midst of their gaiety and laughter, however, Jesus gets serious. He says, "Upon this Rock I will build my church." What kind of church is Jesus hoping to build on the sinking Rock of Peter?

Could it be that *right failure* is more important to Jesus than *right belief*? If so, there would be vast implications not only for the community that bears his name but for any of us who seek to follow in Jesus' footsteps.

So often Christians seem to feel it is their responsibility to build the church on a firm and unshakable foundation. They erect towers and build dogmas and theologies that are meant to stand for all time, for all people, in all places. They expect their followers to grant their unwavering ascent to unchanging creeds and infallible Scriptures. They demand that their adherents sacrifice their intelligence and dignity upon the altar of unquestioning certitude. As a reward for their sacrifice, adherents are promised lives that are as firm and unshakable as their churches supposedly are. Their marriages will last forever and their children will never get into trouble. Their fortunes will be made—and kept—and neither their jobs nor their 401k savings will ever be lost. When you read the fine print on this agreement, however, you discover that an even more troubling assumption is being made: that failure and misfortune are considered signs of God's displeasure and punishment for unfaithfulness. Really?

Jesus seems to want to build his church on a *sinking* rock. When you are upwardly mobile and life has not hit you hard lately, it is easy to assume that you have arrived right where life wants you to be and that all good things will last. We all fall into this trap now and again no matter how many times reality has caught up and shown us otherwise. Sometimes it takes a journey into darkness, even deep darkness, to finally awaken to the smallness of our success-based world. Sometimes you need to lose your way in order to discover the grandeur, mystery, and freedom of the world that awaits you. Sometimes, even, you need to step away from the security of your boat onto the stormy sea of your own awakening to discover that a sinking stone is a far firmer foundation than you have imagined.

THE DARK WOOD

In this book I argue that the surest context for such awakening and discovery is found in the most unlikely and misunderstood of places: a place known most famously (or infamously) as the Dark Wood. Thanks to the Italian poet and moral philosopher Dante Alighieri, the Dark Wood has been misunderstood in the West for the better part of the last millennium as a place to be feared and avoided. In his most famous work, *La divina commedia* (*The Divine Comedy*), Dante wrote allegorically of a Dark Wood he entered at the midpoint of his life where "the true way was wholly lost."[1] In Dante's understanding, the Dark Wood is a place of confusion, emptiness, and stumbling that is entered because of our sin and is inhabited by strange and terrifying denizens. You don't step into the Dark Wood if you don't have to. According to Dante, it marks the entrance to the Inferno and everlasting torment.

Yet, Dante represented a side of the Christian tradition that understood Peter to be the firm, unshakable foundation of the church, not a sinking stone. His conclusions about the Dark Wood were influenced by his underlying assumptions. Another side of the tradition, represented especially by the ancient Christian mystics, understood struggle not as punishment for sin, but as the central context in which revelation takes place. Consequently they remembered and experienced the Dark Wood differently. While the Dark Wood was called by various names by the mystics—Saint John of the Cross called it the dark night of the soul, Saint Teresa of Avila called it the fifth mansion, Dionysus the Areopagite called it the cloud of unknowing—all of them insisted that the Dark Wood is a place where one receives strange and wondrous gifts whose value vastly exceeds whatever hardships are encountered there. The Dark Wood is *where you meet God.*

The mystics taught that in the Dark Wood you discover who you are and what your life is about, flaws and all. Just as I found that my "fat little belly" allowed me the buoyancy I needed to float effortlessly on the surface of Easedale Tarn, so in the Dark Wood you bring all your shortcomings with you, not in order to purge them or be judged by them, but to embrace them in such a way that your struggles contribute meaningfully to the central conversation God is inviting you to have with life.

This book will trace seven unusual gifts found in the Dark Wood. These gifts have been recognized throughout the ages but have been largely lost on modern society in its fear of heading precisely into the territory we will be exploring:

- emptiness
- uncertainty
- getting lost
- being thunderstruck
- temptation
- disappearing
- becoming a misfit

These gifts may appear more like curses than blessings. Certainly they did to Dante. Yet before you dismiss them out of hand, ask yourself, "Do I ever experience any of these?" Some people find themselves in the Dark Wood when they wake up one day and realize that the career that has provided a healthy paycheck for years has also been sucking the life out of them. Others find themselves there when tragedy strikes, or a marriage fails, or a serious health threat arises, shaking their confidence in God's goodness or God's very existence. Some enter the Dark Wood when their beliefs—or doubts—set them at odds with their friends or faith community. They can no longer bring themselves to pray the prayers or recite the creeds because their internal dissonance meter has gone off the charts. For these or other reasons they grow weary of juggling all the masks they wear to project a certain image to the world that has little to do with who they really are. For still others, sheer exhaustion places them in the Dark Wood. They wake up one day facing too many commitments made to too many people, feeling trapped in a tightly woven web of obligation and guilt. If any of these experiences describe you, then if the mystics are right, you are in the best possible position to experience profound awakening and insight about who you are and what you are doing here.

You may find it strange that Dark Wood experiences could bear gifts or blessings that enable you to find your path, but it is part of life's generosity. How nice to know that you don't have to be a saint to find your place in this world! You don't even have to be "above average." All you really need to be is *struggling*.

Incidentally, even the great saints of old experienced significant doubts and struggled with imperfections. They did not become saints by moving from uncertainty to clarity. They moved, rather, from uncertainty to *trust*, which requires the ongoing presence of uncertainty. Likewise, while many saints experienced small and large victories over the course of their lives, they moved not from failure to success, but from failure to *faithfulness*, which requires the ongoing possibility of failure.

One of the great lessons you learn in the Dark Wood is that struggle and challenge provide one of the most reliable contexts in which to discover your path in life, or find your way back when lost. If you're paying attention rather than looking for the nearest way out of the Dark Wood, you discover that your way forward is revealed by a special set of markers, which I like to call "sweet spot" moments.

Golf clubs, baseball and cricket bats, and tennis rackets all have sweet spots. Human lives do, too. The sweet spot on a tennis racket is that place near the center of the strings where the vibrations transmitted through the impact of the ball cancel themselves out, making players nearly unaware that the impact has occurred. Hitting the sweet spot, therefore, feels natural and almost effortless. It allows the players to invest their energies into playing the game, not merely hitting the ball. As effortless as it feels, however, the sweet spot is difficult to locate and hit regularly. A player must practice hard, paying careful attention to how each swing feels under changing conditions, most especially the pressure of competition. Just as the sweet spot of a racket is found by adjusting to continuous impacts made by a ball moving in the opposite direction, so your internal sweet spot tends to be revealed though direct challenge. You keep adjusting your responses until they begin coming from a place where you feel most fully yourself—most fully free, yet wholeheartedly engaged and alive.

In his book *Toward God*, Michael Casey compares the sense of freedom and aliveness one experiences in a sweet-spot moment to a rubber ball that is released after being held under water:

> A rubber ball held under water submits. Once released, it
> springs to the surface; and the deeper it is held, the more

it strains to rise. The human spirit possesses natural buoyancy. It can be held down by enslavement to the senses, by acquisitiveness and ambition, by anger and violence, or by what the New Testament calls "cares." It can be held down, but its natural tendency remains dramatically oriented toward God. It can never be satisfied until this upward impulse is allowed freedom.[2]

If your inner-self, or soul, can be compared to Casey's rubber ball being held under water, you could say that it is yearning to rise to the place where its native buoyancy wants to take it. At no time are you more aware of your native buoyancy than when something deep within you feels like it is being prevented from coming up for air. In the context of your experiences of challenge and struggle within the Dark Wood of life, sweet-spot moments act like homing signals indicating your internal true north. In this respect, the Dark Wood is a sacred space where you not only meet God, but meet yourself—your true self that is most directly connected to, and in conversation with, the divine.

THE MYTHOLOGICAL IMAGINATION AND *THE UNEXPECTED LOVE*

As we explore the Dark Wood, I'll serve as an interpretive guide of sorts. While I take up this task as an ordained Christian minister with twenty years of experience serving churches, you will not find any attempt made to convert you to Christian faith. If I attempt any conversion, it will not be to make you a believer, but to convert you to being more fully *yourself*, as you were created to be. Along the way, we will benefit from insight and wisdom found in a variety of faith traditions, particularly the mythological imagination found within ancient Judaism and Christianity.

By *mythological imagination* I mean stories that have been passed down through the ages not because they happened long ago, but because they *keep happening* all the time, on up to the present. The story of Peter sinking in the Sea of Galilee, for instance, is not just Peter's story but our own, at least at times. By locating ourselves within these stories, we discover that our lives are more intimately bound up in God's story than we ever realized. And because we are bound up in God's story, there is hope beyond our failures and struggles. In fact, our failures and struggles themselves may become our most powerful allies in becoming most fully alive.

Another powerful ally you will encounter regularly in this book is the Holy Spirit. One of the liabilities of using religious language to describe spiritual experience is the baggage it tends to carry. Perhaps no two words in the English language carry more baggage than *Holy Spirit*. Depending on your previous life experiences, particularly those that may intersect fundamentalist religion in some way, what comes to mind when you encounter the name *Holy Spirit* may be very different from what I have in mind, even the exact opposite.

Many Christians believe that the Holy Spirit is their exclusive possession and therefore only they can have access to the Spirit. This belief rests on the dubious assumption that human beings can "possess" the Spirit (we are more likely *possessed by* the Spirit). It also runs contrary to certain Christian Scriptures themselves. In the Gospel of John, for instance, the Holy Spirit is called God's *Logos* or "Divine Word" through whom "everything came into being" and apart from whom "nothing came into being" (John 1:2-3). Jesus is said to be God's *Logos*-made-flesh, literally the *embodiment* of the Holy Spirit. In other words, John's Gospel envisions all of God's creation as intrinsically in relationship with the Holy Spirit. Whether or not God's creations (including human beings) are aware of their connection with the Spirit is another story altogether! Sometimes what is most hidden from our view is right before our eyes.

In the ancient Christian Celtic tradition, every person was believed to be intrinsically connected to the divine through the Holy Spirit, whether Christian or not. Therefore every person was thought to bear the light of God, if only faintly. Under the influence of the Gospel of John, the ninth-century Celtic saint John Scotus Eriugena contended that God did not create everything out of nothing, but out of God's own essence. Therefore, God's essence could be detected in all things, human and nonhuman. This understanding rang true with earlier Christians as well, including Saint Augustine who claimed that the path of knowing oneself and the path to knowing God are one and the same path. Augustine did not believe that human beings define God. Rather, he believed that God defines human beings. "You have made us for yourself, O Lord," writes Augustine, "and our hearts are restless until they find their rest in you."[3] Human restlessness is a sign of our connection to the Holy Spirit. Are you restless?

Perkins School of Theology professor Jack Levison once had a conversation with his students about who the Holy Spirit is, why the Spirit matters, and how to go about experiencing the Spirit. The responses of his students were typical of many of us. One student talked about experiencing the Holy Spirit at a campfire at the end of a week. Another talked about a special worship service. One by one, says Levison, the students said they associate the Spirit with exceptional things in their lives—things that don't normally happen. Our basic problem with the Holy Spirit, he argues, is that we need to take it "from the mountain top and put it into our daily lives."[4]

The great contemplative mystic Thomas Merton was once asked—one too many times—about his life and practices at his hermitage at The Abbey of Gethsemane in Kentucky. Tersely Merton responded, "What I wear is pants. What I do is live. How I pray is breathe."[5] Merton's observation may betray a note of exasperation, but it also reveals his wisdom. For Merton, experiencing the Holy Spirit is not confined to the mountaintop. It is a daily experience. Even a moment-by-moment experience. To Merton, the Holy Spirit is as present—and constant—as breathing.

In the Old Testament, the words for spirit, soul, and breath are related. The Hebrew word for "breath" is the same as the word for "spirit." The Hebrew word for "soul" or "being" may be translated as "breath" as well. Thus in Genesis 2, God is said to have breathed the "breath" (Hebrew: *nephesh*) of life into Adam's nostrils, and Adam became a living "soul/being" (Hebrew: *nephesh*).

This overlapping relationship carries forward into the New

Testament as well, with the Greek word *pneuma*. You can only tell by the context whether *pneuma* means "breath" or "spirit." Even then, it may be unclear. In the Gospel of John, Jesus appears to the disciples after the resurrection then breathes on them saying, "Receive the Holy Spirit" (Greek *pneuma*; John 20:21-22). Did Jesus say "Receive the *Holy Spirit*" or "Receive the *holy breath*"? If we take the biblical relationship between breath and spirit seriously, the answer to both questions just might be yes.

It has been estimated that all of us regularly breathe in at least one molecule of air that Jesus himself once breathed. While that molecule of air is no different from any other air molecule, I love how the awareness of that molecule reengages us with the ancient imagination of the Scriptures. Perhaps our awareness turns receiving Jesus' holy breath into an openness to receiving the Holy Spirit, which in turn allows the Spirit to be as present in our lives as breath itself.

My favorite name for the Holy Spirit is *The Unexpected Love*. You may find my use of the word *unexpected* to be a bit, well, unexpected given that I have just compared the Holy Spirit to breath. Yet consider: today you will take 23,000 to 26,000 breaths of air. When was the last time you *noticed* you were breathing? Proximity and constancy do not often increase awareness but decrease it. Like breathing, we usually don't notice the Spirit acting in our lives until we start paying attention. At the moment we become aware that the Spirit is stirring within us, we tend also to become aware that the Spirit has been stirring us for some time, quietly provoking sweet-spot moments that we have been too distracted to notice.

The Holy Spirit tends to catch us by surprise, therefore, not so much because the Spirit comes and goes, but because our awareness does. As the Latin proverb popularized by Carl Jung reminds us, "Bidden or unbidden, God is present."[6] When unbidden, the Spirit tends to catch us unprepared. No matter how many times the Spirit has knocked at my door, when I open that door I'm startled all over again. "Oh, it's you! I didn't think *you* were coming," or "Oh, it's you! I thought you were the gardener," or "If I'd have known *you* were coming to dinner, I might have straightened up the house first."

Showing up for dinner is perhaps more apt a metaphor than it seems. In Luke 14, Jesus noticed how guests at a dinner party sought out the best seats at the table. In response, he offered his disciples advice that serves as one of the best—and most commonly overlooked—descriptions I know of regarding how the Holy Spirit quietly meets us in our everyday lives.

In Jesus' day, positions around a dinner table were arranged according to the relative status of each guest. Guests held in highest honor sat closest to the host while seats at the far end of the table were reserved for those held in least esteem. This custom may sound unfair, but in ancient times it was a way of ensuring that your neighbor didn't steal your goat or cause you any other harm that might lead to public humiliation each time people gathered for a common meal.

When invited to dinner, Jesus advises his disciples not to assume the most honorable seats. For "someone more highly regarded than you could have been invited by your host. The host who invited both of you will come and say to you, 'Give your seat to this other person.' Embarrassed, you will take your seat in the least important place."

Instead, Jesus advises his disciples to take the least important place. Then, "when your host approaches you, he will say, 'Friend, move up here at a better seat.' Then you will be honored in the presence of all your fellow guests" (Luke 14:7-10).

Given Jesus' advice, where do you suppose he himself sat when invited to dinner? I'm guessing he sat with the riffraff at the far end unless his host specifically invited him to sit higher.

When I consider my experience of the Holy Spirit, Jesus' simple advice seems like more than just a reflection on Ancient Near Eastern table manners. All of us are a bit like walking dinner conversations. Around our internal table, a number of voices sit, rarely ceasing to offer their opinion about whatever decision confronts us. How many distinct voices can you find? I don't know about you, but I hear plenty of opinions expressed inside my head when simply choosing a restaurant to which to take an out-of-town guest, let alone the cacophony that erupts when making weightier decisions, like choosing a vocational direction or selecting between candidates for a job. "How about taking your guests to that really swanky restaurant down the road?" one voice suggests. Another immediately counters, "That place is too expensive!" To which another voice replies straight out of *Ferris Bueller's Day Off,* "Come on, live a little!" Still another voice quietly asks, "What kind of food do *your guests* enjoy?"

I don't know how often the Holy Spirit is inclined to weigh in on my restaurant choices, but I do know that when it comes to making decisions that truly affect my life's path—or the path of others—the Holy Spirit always has an opinion. But do I listen?

Often, I've placed too many other conversation partners around my internal table, a lot closer to my ear. They argue. They shout over one another. They wave their hands trying to get my attention. They get upset if I'm paying too much attention to another voice. But the Holy Spirit, like Jesus himself, tends to prefer sitting quietly down at the far end of the table—perfectly content to let the conversation roll on without trying to barge in.

It's not that the Holy Spirit isn't interested in helping me. The Spirit simply isn't one to strong-arm a conversation or offer advice I don't truly want to hear. In fact, the Spirit seems perfectly content to remain silent until or unless I care enough to rearrange the seating order. Even then, the Spirit usually speaks in whispers (a "still small voice" as the prophet Elijah put it—1 Kings 19:12 KJV). So I've got to send my ego down to the far end of the table. I seat my inner child (sometimes wonderfully free, sometimes a spoiled brat) a little lower, too. Same for my inner parent, my pessimist and pragmatist friends, and even my heroes. When these voices and many others have finally assumed their proper positions, and the Spirit is next to my ear, I tend to hear the Spirit's voice most clearly. The advice I receive is often surprising.

I'm convinced that it was a surprising, counterintuitive voice of the Spirit that led to the creation of this book. For this is *not* the book I had originally intended to write.

My original plan was to write a book based on my doctoral dissertation at Princeton Theological Seminary. Shortly after my dissertation was published in 1997, I received interest from a noted academic publisher who sought to publish a revised version in a prestigious series of scholarly monographs. The next several years were spent revising it on study-leaves from my church. In the end, I could never reach agreement with the editors on certain sections of the book, so the manuscript sat in my closet until, a decade later, a minister colleague suggested I turn the manuscript into a book intended for a lay audience.

"That's brilliant!" I exclaimed, wondering why the thought had never occurred to me before. Immediately, I made plans to spend some time at a retreat center in Arizona to get a start on the manuscript. I excitedly announced my plans to my Omaha congregation before leaving, explaining how it had been my dream for years to publish the book and how thrilled I was by the prospect of people I actually served—laypeople, not scholars—benefitting from it.

Arriving at Spirit of the Desert Retreat Center in Carefree, Arizona, in the spring of 2010, I set out a large pile of note cards I'd prepared, anxious to create my masterpiece and bring closure to years of disappointment with the scholarly route to publication. "This will be the easiest book I've ever written," I told myself. How could it not be? I'd revised my dissertation four times for the academic publisher before giving up on it.

At the retreat center I anxiously sat down at my computer and waited for the muse to take me. And waited some more. Nothing came. Nervously fumbling with my notecards, the voices in my head were all trying to offer their "helpful" advice. "Start with this one!" "No, start here and take it in this direction." "Are you kidding? You should try this." I made attempt after attempt simply to write the first chapter—and eventually *any* chapter—trying to find the slightest toehold from which to gain firmer footing. By the end of the first week, all the voices inside me reached complete agreement: "This book isn't going *anywhere!*"

In complete despair, I sat on the floor with all my notecards carefully arranged in a large circle around me and prayed: "What on earth would you have me do, God? I'm writing this book for *you*, and thus far you haven't helped me *at all!*"

There was no response.

After a half hour, I tried another angle. "You know, don't you, that I've only got a week left to get a start on this book? The way things are going, I'll be returning to Omaha with nothing but my tail between my legs. I know you have me here to write a book. *So why don't you help?*"

Still nothing.

Finally, gathering up all my carefully arranged notecards in my hands, I prayed, "If it be your will, I'm ready to trash this whole book. If this isn't the book I should write, then I'm willing to return to Omaha and tell my congregation that it was all for nothing. I'd rather be embarrassed than try to write something you don't want me to write."

"Are you sure?" came the immediate response.

"Yes, down to the depths of my soul, I'm sure. I'll throw away everything if that's what you want."

"Good. Now that I finally have your full attention: *I don't want you to write that book.* I've been trying all this time to get you to write a *different* book."

Bewildered, I asked, "What do you want me to write about?"

"I'm glad you asked."

Almost immediately, my mind was flooded with intuitions—words, thoughts, visual images that all had a particular coherence to them. They broke loose like a river whose waters had been long-blocked by debris and were now racing unencumbered toward the sea.

The coherent thought behind those intuitions could be expressed this way: "I want you to write about *your relationship with me.* Write about your struggle to hear my voice over the years and what you've learned through those struggles. Write about how to seek and find my guidance in life's Dark Wood."

Over the course of the next week, my heart sang as I wrote almost without effort until the early morning hours each day. The biggest obstacle I encountered had nothing to do with writing. It was dealing with my continual laughter at myself: "How is it that a person writing about being guided by the Holy Spirit could have been so deaf to the Spirit's invitation to write about being guided by the Spirit?!" I laughed (rather than cried) because the answer was implicit in the question: this is how it works for all of us. Even the great saints of old all struggled to discern the Spirit's voice from all the others around their internal table. Yet just as my experience at that Arizona retreat center proved all over again, if there is a will, the Spirit makes a way. And the Spirit's way is frequently *unexpected.*

Part of what it means to seek the Holy Spirit's guidance in life's

Dark Wood is to learn how to rearrange the seating arrangement at your inner dinner table on a daily basis in order to hear the Spirit's quiet, unassuming whispers. Then, like Peter, you are invited to get up and step out on the stormy sea in response to the Spirit's call. I do not watch for apparitions of Jesus, or the clouds to part or a shaft of light to suddenly stream from the heavens when the Spirit calls, nor do I expect a booming voice to sound from on high. In my experience the Spirit's voice is more likely to be carried along by inner hunches, sweet-spot moments, and subtle intuitions that gently click something into place that had been out of alignment. Like Peter, too, I have learned that sometimes failure can be a friend. Failure can indicate that something is going right, not wrong.

In my Dark Wood wandering over the years I have found that these hunches, intuitions, and sweet-spot moments are like the breath of the Holy Spirit. They come regularly, but almost always take me by surprise because of their quiet constancy. When I become aware of the Spirit's voice, I pay close attention, for I have learned that the Spirit knows me better than *I* know me. When the Spirit stirs the deepest waters within me, I discover—and begin to claim—my true self as well as the connection I share with others. I move another step toward becoming the person I was created to be. One who is most fully alive and fully at home in this world—more like a living human being than like Pinocchio.

This book is for all Dark Wood wanderers who seek to find themselves, and *The Unexpected Love* in the heart of their everyday struggles.

2

THE GIFT OF UNCERTAINTY

Certainty is overrated.

—Brian McLaren

To imply that you enter the Dark Wood of your own volition is a bit of a misnomer. One thing Dante got right is that you *awaken* there. ("I awoke in a Dark Wood where the true way was wholly lost.") Sometimes, even, you are pushed there. The reason Dante gives for finding yourself in the Dark Wood—sin—is absolutely wrong, however, or at least doesn't begin to tell the full story. What sets you in the Dark Wood is awakening itself—an awakening provoked by the sometimes gentle, sometimes not-so-gentle, nudge of the Holy Spirit.

As the ancients knew well, you may enter the Dark Wood through the "path of glory" or the "path of despair." It may be through an ecstatic experience of profound awe and wonder as happened to the apostle Paul on the road to Damascus, or through a life crisis as happened to Dante at the midpoint of his life. Most of us follow Dante's route. Once you find yourself in the Dark Wood, however, it seems far less relevant which path you took before you woke up. Awakening is awakening.

From the moment you realize that there is more to life than meets the eye, and that you are as much a mystery to yourself as to anyone else, and that the mystery that is you longs more than anything else to connect with the mystery of God, you have entered the Dark Wood. What keeps you in the Dark Wood is a developing sense of God's presence in the darkness. You may not name this presence "God," especially at first. You may simply become aware that you are experiencing sweet-spot moments where something clicks into place in a way that feels most natural. Or you may experience moments where you feel a rising within you much like a rubber ball held under water being released. Something inside cries "Home!" and yearns to move in a particular direction. If you pay attention to these moments, you find that they have a similar quality to them. When you connect the dots, they point in a certain direction inviting you to follow. They mark your path forward, or a portion of it anyway.

These experiences, or "touches" of the Holy Spirit, have a way of exciting and perhaps terrifying you at the same time. The excitement comes from the sense that they are inviting you to a place, or a life, that is far more wonderful than you have imagined. The terror comes from this very realization. You *haven't* imagined it. At least you haven't *seriously* imagined it, though you may have been dreaming about it for years. Since you hadn't been planning on heading in this particular direction, you feel woefully ill prepared for the journey.

Likely, therefore, you will resist the direction that these sweet-spot moments indicate. This is to be expected whenever a person senses a call to inhabit their place in the world. If the source of the call is truly coming from a power higher than yourself, it means that it is calling you forward based on far greater information and awareness than you can possess on your own. It sees further down the path than you do. The call of the Holy Spirit, as inviting as it is, also tends to shake things up and bears with it a particular Dark Wood gift: the gift of *uncertainty*.

To most people, uncertainty seems more like a curse than a gift. When you cannot see the endpoint of your journey, or the path ahead is not clearly marked, you grow nervous. If you do not have rock-solid assurances that everything will be OK and that the path ahead is perfectly safe, you tend to dig your heels in.

Yet religion does a disservice when it seeks to remove uncertainty from life. Have you ever noticed how the more certainty a religion claims to deliver, the more frenzied and hysterical are its adherents? The fact of the matter is that life is messy and no amount of doctrine or dogma changes this. Faith built upon certainty is a house of cards that falls apart when the "unshakable foundation" shifts even slightly.

Curiously, insofar as Judaism and Christianity are concerned, *all* of the heroes of both the Old and New Testaments lived in the midst of high uncertainty. Whether you look at Moses, Abraham, or King David in the Old Testament Scriptures, or Peter, Paul, or even Jesus in the New Testament, there is no evidence to suggest that faith exempted them from uncertainty and struggle. In fact, the only people who consider certainty and absence of struggle to be a high value in the Bible are the *villains*. From the serpent in the garden of Eden enticing the original couple with the absolute knowledge of good and evil, to Pontius Pilate who crucified Jesus in exchange for assurance of remaining in power a little longer, the Jewish and Christian Scriptures continually portray certainty as highly overrated. Even dangerous.

According to the apostle Paul, those of us who have a high need for certainty in life are being childish. While certainty may come in the fullness of time, to have an adult faith is to put away our desire for certainty. Says Paul, "When I was a child, I spoke like a child, I thought like a child, I reasoned like a child; when I became an adult, I put an end to childish ways. For now we see in a mirror, dimly, but then we will see face to face. Now I know only in part; then I will know fully, even as I have been fully known" (1 Corinthians 13:11-12 NRSV).

Of course, children do enjoy a degree of uncertainty as long as the outcome doesn't really matter. They love to turn the crank on a jack-in-the-box and be surprised when jack jumps out. But once you turn to more serious matters—like replacing their usual blue sippy cup with a green one—all hell breaks loose! Children love certainty and crave black-and-white dependability.

The word translated as "dimly" in the passage above comes from the Greek word *anigmati*. *Anigmati* is where the English word *enigma* comes from. What's an enigma? Enigma means "mystery." Enigma is "puzzling, a riddle, ambiguous, difficult to understand or interpret." What Paul is saying is that a mature faith is one that embraces life as a mystery to be lived, not a problem to be solved—that accepts uncertainty as a gift, not a curse.

Imagine going to a movie that's totally predictable. When is the last time you have enjoyed such a film since childhood? Do you give high marks to films where the protagonists are certain about the future, know exactly how to respond in every situation, and always succeed in carrying out whatever they set their mind to? These are the films that score 20 out of 100 in the Rotten Tomato ratings. We may not need bombs exploding or cars crashing to be engaged with a film, but we do need uncertainty. We become especially interested when people are faced with difficult challenges and are forced to make choices when neither we, nor they, can predict the outcome.

Yet I must confess that if I were given the opportunity to write the script of my own life, my first inclination would be to fill it with highly predictable outcomes, constant success, and no significant challenges. Every book I set about writing would become a *New York Times* best seller, every sermon would move my congregation to tears, my wife, Melanie, would laugh at all my jokes, and our daughters would think I'm the coolest dad who ever walked the earth. Yet I would never pay a dime to watch such a film, not even of my own life. So if I wouldn't want to watch this film, why would I want to live this life?

Too much certainty removes the adventure from life and sucks the joy out of relationships. When a marriage becomes predictable, love wanes. Couples seek counseling or even get divorced. The strongest relationships are those where each partner continues to experience mystery and new awareness concerning the other. As a friend of mine observed, "I've been married to twenty-nine different women in thirty years. Coincidentally, each of them happened to be named Marianna!"

If we are to live an engaging life, and remain engaged with others, we need something greater than certainty as a foundation. As author John Ortberg observes in his book *Faith and Doubt*, "We all think we want certainty. But we don't. What we really want is trust, wisely placed. Trust is better than certainty because it honors the freedom of persons and makes possible growth and intimacy that certainty alone could never produce."[1]

Seen from this perspective, it is no coincidence that the apostle Paul's observation about embracing uncertainty comes on the heels of one of the greatest passages about love in the entire Bible—one that is read in countless weddings every day. "If I...do not have love, I am a noisy gong or a clanging symbol" (1 Corinthians 13:1). The greatest way to kill love is to take the adventure out of it, and there's nothing better at killing adventure than suffocating it with certainty.

Paul understands that love thrives in *un*certainty—not the kind of uncertainty that increases chaos, but the kind that develops trust. It is trust developed in the caldron of uncertainty that not only makes passionate lovers out of two individuals but also gives us the confidence to allow the sweet-spot moments of our lives to lead us more deeply into the Dark Wood and find our place in this world.

STEPPING INTO THE WATER

For many years I have been an avid reader of the British poet David Whyte. Before devoting his life to poetry, Whyte tells of a period when his soul felt trapped in a prison cell of certainty and predictability. Having moved to the United States, he began working for a small nonprofit organization in the Pacific Northwest. He believed strongly in the organization's mission and was pleased for a time to lend his efforts to helping them achieve it. Yet as weeks turned into months, the seemingly infinite administrative tasks and details of his work began to wear away his enthusiasm. Whyte's interest in his work gradually withered, and with it, his energy and patience. Eventually, it was only his stalwart belief in the organization's cause that kept him trudging to work each day. Feeling increasingly worn down and imprisoned by his work, Whyte remembers a pivotal conversation with friend and Benedictine monk, David Steindl-Rast:

"Brother David? . . . Tell me about exhaustion."

"He looked at me with an acute, searching, compassionate ferocity for the briefest of moments, as if trying to sum up the entirety of the situation and without missing a beat, as if he had been waiting all along to say a life-changing thing to me. He said, in the form both of a question and an assertion:

"You know that the antidote to exhaustion is not necessarily rest?"

. . . "What is it, then?"

"The antidote to exhaustion is *wholeheartedness*....

"You are so tired through and through because a good half of what you do here in this organization has nothing to do with your true powers, or the place you have reached in your life. You are only half here, and half here will kill you after a while. You need something to which you can give your full powers. You know what that is; I don't have to tell you."

[Pointing to the poem Whyte had just been reading by Rainer Maria Rilke about a swan, Brother David continued.] "You are like Rilke's Swan in his awkward waddling across the ground; the swan doesn't cure his awkwardness by beating himself on the back, by moving faster, or by trying to organize himself better. He does it by moving toward the elemental water, where he belongs. It is the simple contact with the water that gives him grace and presence. You only have to touch the elemental waters in your own life, and it will transform everything. But you have to let yourself down into those waters from the ground on which you stand, and that can be hard. Particularly if you think you might drown....Let go of all this effort, and let yourself down, however awkwardly, into the waters."[2]

Brother David was advising Whyte to replace certainty with trust in those sweet-spot moments that orient you toward your place in the world.

Whether the Spirit's voice comes to you through a quiet and inviting intuition or a sudden jolt of friendly advice, the experience can be uncomfortable. If you've been waddling on dry land for very long, chances are that you've become used to it. However awkward your waddling may feel, it feels normal. Sometimes what is needed is a little shove from the Spirit into those elemental waters to get us swimming.

THE MAN WHO DIDN'T WANT TO BE MADE WELL

There is a frequently misunderstood story in the fifth chapter of John's Gospel about a man who refused to let himself down into those elemental waters—quite literally. Seen from the right angle, the story illustrates the lengths we will go to hold onto our security, and the lengths that the Spirit will go to take it away in order to heal us. It is the story of Jesus' encounter with a man at the pool of Beth-Zatha.

The pool at Beth-Zatha, also known as Bethesda, was a place that, until 1964, many scholars thought was a fiction or at least a pious misunderstanding from an author who may never have lived in Jerusalem. Scholars were doubtful because excavations in Jerusalem failed to uncover any conclusive evidence of the healing pool in our story. Then in 1964, archaeologists uncovered a whole complex of pools and buildings that not only matched the description of the site in John's Gospel but also showed that the site had been considered a holy site by ancient Christians who likely identified them with John's story. The healing that takes place in this story is the only one recorded in the Gospels of a person who *did not want to be healed.* Why would a man who was paralyzed not want to be healed? Read on, and perhaps you will find yourself in the story.

So here's this pool where people have apparently gone for a very long time for healing. Some manuscript traditions include a brief description in John 5 of how healings worked at the pool. They say the waters would occasionally be "troubled" (some manuscripts add "by an angel"). When the waters were troubled, the belief was that the first person into the pool would be healed.

When Jesus visits the pool, he finds this man begging beside it whom Jesus perceives to have been there for a very long time. How would Jesus know this? Some imagine that Jesus read his mind. Yet imagine how you yourself might arrive at a similar conclusion. All the people seem to know this man by name and show deference toward him. He's lying in the prime begging location—a spot surely coveted by the other beggars, none of whom dare to usurp it. These other beggars don't have the seniority. Nor do they have the social capital necessary to oust him from his spot with the support of others. This man clearly rules the roost. Anyone taking more than a minute to observe the situation could have concluded that this man has been there awhile. To acknowledge this doesn't take away from Jesus' power. It simply concedes that Jesus was a careful observer of his surroundings. He took time to look, listen, and notice things that many of us overlook before he acted.

The Gospel writer indicates that the man has been begging beside the pool for thirty-eight years. Jesus approaches him and asks, "Do you *want* to be made well?" *Of course* he does, doesn't he? Curious that the man doesn't lash out, "Why do you think I'm here to begin with?!" Instead, he hems and haws, never providing a direct answer: "Sir, I have no one to put me into the pool when the water is stirred up; and while I am making my way, someone else steps down ahead of me" (vv. 6-7, emphasis added).

Really?

In thirty-eight years this man has yet to be first in the water? Let's assume he's afflicted with an unusually debilitating handicap. Perhaps he can't move himself at all, under his own power. Would it not seem strange that in thirty-eight years no one would have taken pity on him and moved him into the pool? In thirty-eight years, wouldn't the other beggars not have made sure he could be first in the pool if for no other reason than to take over the prime begging spot for themselves? If you believe that this man never had a chance to make it into the pool, I'm sure he would be glad to sell you a bridge from Brooklyn to Jerusalem.

No, this man has no interest in being healed. After all, he's making a good living. He's got the respect of his peers. His social, religious, and economic world revolves around the pool. His life is defined by his limitations. To heal this man would be to disrupt everything he knows and has become accustomed to in this world. *It would take away his certainty.*

But Jesus *does* heal him. "Stand up, take up your mat and walk" (v. 8). And the man jumps up, thanks Jesus profusely with great emotion, and offers to follow him for the rest of his days, right? No! The man takes up his mat and walks away so angry that he never bothers to say thank you or even learn Jesus' name. A short time later, Jesus will find the man in another location—begging as he was before. Jesus calls him out exclaiming, "See, you have been made well! Do not sin any more, so that nothing worse happens to you" (John 5:14 NRSV). At this, the man marches straight to the Pharisees and tries to help them arrest Jesus on the charge that Jesus healed him on the Sabbath and had thus broken the law not to "work."

Why does Jesus bother healing this man who doesn't want to be healed in the first place? Probably for the same reason the Holy Spirit keeps pushing all of us "into places we wouldn't necessarily go ourselves." Jesus knows that the human soul is terrifically buoyant. Its yearning is for the freedom that comes from answering the Spirit's call. Shackled by our fears and excuses for very long, the soul inevitably revolts and seeks to break free. When it wins the revolt, we may find ourselves in places we wouldn't necessarily go ourselves, but we also find that we are terrifically OK with that. We experience a taste of freedom, even joy, like Rilke's swan finding its home in its elemental waters.

At the pool of Beth-Zatha, Jesus knew that the beggar struggled with more than bodily paralysis. He was stricken by the fear of uncertainty. Likely, his hope in healing the man against his will was to awaken and empower the deeper will within him. Tasting true freedom for the first time in thirty-eight years, the man might awaken as if from a long, dull dream to discover that the world was made to be free in. And yes, while the man would have to move from being a beggar at the top of the totem pole, living an utterly predictable life, to struggling (at least for a while) at the bottom end of productive society with no easy certainties, Jesus knew that the man would truly be happier if he awakened because his life would finally be filled with *soul*. Before he died, he would actually experience living, not because he was free of his paralysis, but because he was free of his fear.

DO YOU WANT TO BE HEALED?

In the summer of 2008, my family experienced the most terrifying crisis we have ever faced, on a day that had promised to be one of the most glorious days of our lives. The crisis would plunge us into deep uncertainty about the future and challenge us to face our greatest fears.

I had started a position as the senior minister at Countryside Community Church in Omaha, Nebraska, in April and had been living in Omaha for three months before my family caught up with me from Scottsdale, Arizona. Already, I had fallen in love with my new congregation and its ministry. Now at last the family I loved so much was joining me in Omaha and we were moving into the home of our dreams. It was hard not to feel like we had reached one of life's great "arrival points," where long years of hard work had resulted in a bountiful harvest that might just last for many years to come.

It lasted only a few hours.

In the middle of our move-in day, our seventeen-year-old daughter, Arianna, experienced a pronounced dizzy spell and had to lie down. She had experienced a similar spell earlier that summer, though no one was particularly concerned at the time.

Arianna had been running track in 100-plus-degree Arizona weather and hadn't been drinking enough fluids. Now in Omaha, we became concerned. We decided to play it "ultra-safe" and take Arianna to the emergency room to be checked out.

When the ER doctor informed us of Arianna's MRI results, Melanie and I heard what no parent ever expects to hear about their child: "There is an abnormality in your daughter's brain scan." After more testing, the "abnormality" turned out to be a malignant brain tumor known as an *astrocytoma*.

Suddenly, what was supposed to be one of life's peak moments collapsed into a deep abyss, shaking all of us to our core. Arianna would need to undergo brain surgery as soon as possible to remove what they could of the tumor. The twelve-hour surgery resulted in the extraction of just a little over half the tumor, and it was determined that Arianna would need to undergo a second surgery in the hopes that more could be removed. Only, we were told in advance that Arianna's tumor was not one that could be removed entirely.

Needless to say, our family experienced the kinds of thoughts and emotions you might imagine someone in our position would experience. Abject terror. Bitter despair. Deep sadness. Rage.

Harder than any of these feelings was the nagging uncertainty we experienced from moment to moment. Would brain surgery leave Arianna physically or mentally impaired? How much of the tumor would ultimately be extracted? What if the tumor grew back? And then there was the question none of us wanted to face: What was Arianna's life expectancy?

Each of us faced our own distinctive set of questions, too. Arianna, of course, was faced most existentially with the question of her own mortality and the prospect of permanent physical or mental deficits. Our daughter Maren, age fifteen, wrestled with feelings of guilt over the fact that she was perfectly healthy while her sister suffered. Melanie and I wrestled with how to be supportive parents for both girls, and supportive spouses, even as we grappled with our own emotional collapse.

As our family crisis unfolded, the United States was experiencing its own particular crisis: the most catastrophic economic collapse since the Great Depression. Since our Arizona house was still on the market, its value was in free fall, raising the prospect that we would soon lose the equity we had built over thirteen years or even emerge "upside down," jeopardizing our ability to repay the temporary loan we had received to purchase our new home. While these considerations were minor in relation to our larger crisis, they simply reinforced the feeling that every source of stability and certainty in life had been swept out from under our feet—that *we* were in free fall like our Arizona house.

Our new church members were in a bit of a free fall as well, grieving right along with us as we made our way through the darkness, as well as experiencing job losses and uncertainty related to the nation's economic weal and woe. One night, between Arianna's first and second surgeries, I was sitting in a trustees meeting feeling like it was the last place I wanted to be. They were discussing the potential effects of the economic collapse on our pledge campaign. While there was no hard evidence that Countryside was in immediate danger (our campaign had only just begun) I felt like

I was sitting in a room full of Chicken Littles, convinced that the sky was falling—right on top of Countryside Community Church!

I thought to myself, *How can you be so worked up about scenarios that haven't even happened when, even if they did happen, they would deprive us only of money, not life itself—like my family is facing?*

As the trustees droned on and on about what "could" or "might" or "probably will" happen, a thought arose at the back of my mind that came increasingly to the forefront, eventually becoming quite insistent. I wanted to scream: *You have no right to be worrying over anything until it presents itself to be worried about! You're only adding unnecessary fear and stress when some of us have quite enough as it is!*

I paused before speaking out, however, because the message seemed to be pointed at *me* even more than to them. The question Jesus posed to the beggar at the pool at Beth-Zatha seemed to be directed to me in that moment: "Do *you* want to be healed?"

Caught off-guard, it quickly dawned on me that what the trustees were doing with respect to their imagined financial crisis was what I had been doing in my imagination over the possible results of Arianna's health crisis. I was making myself sick over all the horrors that *might* happen long before they ever *could* happen.

My constant anxieties were helping no one. If anything, they were causing me to retreat within myself. Wrapped up as I was spinning endless future scenarios, I was too emotionally drained to be fully present in the real situation in front of me—not for my daughters, my wife, or my congregation.

I resisted this awkward view of myself at first. "Isn't a father *supposed* to worry?" Letting go of any amount of fear felt like betrayal of my daughter—like I would be backing away as Arianna wrestled with her own fear and uncertainty.

"Arianna needs to let go, as well" is what I heard. "How will you help her reclaim her life if your heart is broken over things that are not yet broken—and may never be?"

From that moment forward, I determined to accept the message as a personal mantra: "Do not worry about anything until it presents itself to be worried about." It has been a mantra ever since—applied to *all* forms of uncertainty, not just Arianna's. It gave me my life back and helped the rest of the family regain theirs.

Our family has been fortunate. Arianna emerged from two brain surgeries with none of the physical or mental challenges we had feared and lives a healthy, happy, and abled life. None of her subsequent MRIs, which she undergoes twice a year, have ever turned up evidence of growth in the tiny bit of tumor that remains, and Arianna has not only graduated from high school, but college, and now is happily employed in a job she loves and excels at.

Did God play a role in healing our daughter's brain tumor? Frankly, I cannot say for certain, nor do I feel the need to. What is far more certain is that in the heart of our deepest abyss, *The Unexpected Love* showed up. Showed up in the form of meals delivered by people we didn't even know, prayers being offered, and kind words being spoken. This Presence also showed up in the amazing dedication of the many doctors, nurses, and Arianna's chief surgeon, each of whom had devoted their lives to serving patients just like her. The Spirit showed up in the form of Arianna's own courage and resiliency, and her subsequent decision to make the most out of the life she's been given. And the Spirit showed up in the form of a heart that each member of our family now carries that is now large enough to embrace others whose crises may not be the same as ours, but whose journey through the Dark Wood has exposed them to similar vulnerabilities.

I also believe *The Unexpected Love* showed up within me just as I had become most withdrawn, whispering that quiet message about worrying. In this message, now a regular mantra, the Spirit taught me about uncertainty's greatest gift: uncertainty teaches us to let go of all concerns but the ones we truly face, giving us the courage and power to face them. In so doing, uncertainty provides the unexpected invitation to live our lives *wholeheartedly*.

3

THE GIFT OF EMPTINESS

God created the world out of nothing,
and as long as we are nothing,
God can make something out of us.
—Martin Luther

THE DARK WOOD ISN'T JUST A place of darkness. It contains many clearings where the light breaks through, the sun gently warms one's face, and the traveler is caught up in awe-struck reverence over the expansiveness of it all. The thirteenth-century mystic poet Jalāl ad-Dīn Muḥammad Rūmī writes of one such clearing this way:

> *Out beyond ideas of wrongdoing and rightdoing,*
> *there is a field. I'll meet you there.*
> *When the soul lies down in that grass,*
> *the world is too full to talk about.*
> *Ideas, language, even the phrase each other*
> *doesn't make any sense.*[1]

The Dark Wood gift of emptiness brings us straight to this place beyond notions of wrongdoing and rightdoing. It's not a place beyond morality. Rather, it's where our fractured humanity finds its most intimate connection to divinity and an astonishing fullness is discovered within our deepest emptiness.

RABBI ELIEZER'S PARADOX

This paradox is explored in a story I heard from a friend long ago of two groups of rabbis who were fiercely at odds over the nature of our relationship to the divine: are human beings separate from God such that God might be considered wholly other than ourselves? Or, are we connected to God in such a way that human beings might be considered manifestations of God?

After arguing for years without resolution, one rabbi suggested they make the long and arduous journey to seek an audience with the great and wise Rabbi Eliezer. It was a rare opportunity to be granted an audience with the famed rabbi because he spent so much time in prayer and meditation and because so many sought his advice. As sharply divided as the rabbis were over their question, making the journey was something everyone could agree on. They all vowed to accept whatever verdict Rabbi Eliezer might render.

Happily for the rabbis, their journey was made without incident and they were granted an audience with Rabbi Eliezer a week after their arrival. When the day came, both groups nervously shuffled into Rabbi Eliezer's private audience chamber. A representative of the first group approached Rabbi Eliezer, bowed low, and presented his group's case, that God is wholly other than ourselves.

The great rabbi listened attentively. Then, he slowly stroked his beard and considered the representative's argument as everyone patiently waited. Suddenly, the rabbi sat straight up in his chair, eyes bright with excitement, and declared, "You're right!"

Hearing this, the second group erupted in protest. "How can this be? You haven't even heard our side yet!"

"Very well," Rabbi Eliezer conceded, "make your case." A representative of the second group came forward and argued passionately regarding our essential unity with God. Again, a prolonged silence ensued as the great rabbi stroked his beard and considered their argument. Then, he sat straight up in his chair, eyes bright with exhilaration, and declared, "You're right!"

Hearing this, the first group rose in protest. "But rabbi," they argued, "you just said, 'You're right!' to *both* groups!"

Once again, the rabbi stroked his beard as he considered their protest. Finally, eyes beaming with revelation, Rabbi Eliezer stood up and declared, "You're right!" And thus his audience with the rabbis was concluded.

The story of Rabbi Eliezer's Paradox points to something real about our relationship with God that cannot be grasped using the tools of logic and argumentation. Like stumbling into an open field in the middle of the Dark Wood, we don't find ourselves there by way of maps but experience. The experience that brings us there is one of emptiness before it is one of fullness. We must first experience the "wholly otherness" of God before we encounter God within us.

WHOLLY HUMAN

"Let me begin by telling you a little about yourself," writes author and Unitarian minister Forrest Church in the preface to his book *Lifecraft*.

To one extent or another the following is true:

You are self-conscious about your appearance.

You feel guilty about things you have done or failed to do.

You sometimes have a hard time accepting yourself or forgiving others.

You are insecure sexually.

You are a less-than-perfect parent, or a less-than-perfect child of imperfect parents, or both.

You are a frustrated husband, wife, or partner, or you are frustrated not to be a husband, wife, or partner.

You have secrets, which you might betray, or which might betray you, at any moment.

However successful you are, you fail in ways that matter both to you and to your loved ones.

Beyond all this, your life is stressful, your happiness fleeting, your health insecure.

You worry about aging.

You sometimes worry about dying.

More than once your heart has been broken by betrayal or loss.

And however successful you may be, however deep

your faith, when the roof caves in, you shake your fist at heaven, the fates, or life itself.

You beg for an answer to the question "Why"—"Why this? Why me? Why now?"

You wonder what your life means.[2]

How does Forrest Church know us so well? Because Forrest Church knew himself so well. It did not matter that Church was a highly successful minister, serving one of the country's preeminent and historic Unitarian churches before he died in 2009. Nor did it matter that Church had a brilliant mind, or that he authored or edited over twenty books. No amount of success, brilliance, or published works exempt you from insecurity and failure, even when you are walking squarely on your life's path. What separated Church from most people was not the fullness of his gifts but his fearlessness in the face of shortcomings—his own shortcomings and those of others. Few people have the courage to squarely face their inner emptiness, like Church did.

Imagine what it would be like to be free—free not of your faults but your *fear* of them. This is precisely what the Dark Wood gift of emptiness brings. One of the strange paradoxes of the gift of emptiness is that it appears to those still standing outside the Dark Wood as a negation of self-worth and identity. Yet the experience of those on the inside is not negation but a fulfillment of these very things. They discover what Jesus meant when he said, "Whoever tries to preserve their life will lose it, but whoever loses their life will preserve it" (Luke 17:33).

45

FEAR VS. FLOW

Operating underneath the surface of Jesus' statement is a movement from fear to flow. Flow is what results when you stop obsessing over your need to survive or be right or be perfect and discover that you have been given distinctive gifts and abilities that bring you alive in this world (and may *keep* you alive here) that are accessible only when you let go of your need for survival, rightness, and perfection. Such gifts are largely invisible when your view is clouded by fear and self-loathing or blaming others.

Not long ago I bent down to examine a small frog that had hopped across my path while walking through a forest. When I drew near, my presence spooked the frog and it hopped away as fast as it could go. The path between the frog and its presumed realm of safety was full of obstacles—twigs, sticks, rocks, grasses—yet I watched in awe as that little frog performed some of the most incredible acrobatics I have ever seen. It twisted, flipped, swung, and rolled so swiftly and gracefully it would have put a Cirque du Soleil performer to shame. I'm not sure it actually happened this way, but I could have sworn it shouted, "Yaaahooo!" in the midst of its escape.

What allowed the frog to escape so quickly and nimbly? Surely, "classic" fear played a certain role, triggering its survival instinct. While fear may have triggered its *instinct* the frog's escape was surely made possible by its *ability*. Its "frogishness." Its *flow*. I'm no biologist, but I would guess that the frog's effortless acrobatics were the result of about one-tenth fear and nine-tenths *flow*. What ensured its deft escape was doing what millions of years of evolution has bred the frog to do naturally. If the ratio of fear to flow had been reversed, it may have responded more like a human being would. It might have cowered and cried, "Woe is to me! I'm just a lowly frog who does not have the size, intelligence, or strength to take on this formidable opponent in my path!" It might even have shook its "fist at heaven, the fates, or life itself" wondering, "Why—Why this? Why me? Why now?" Instead, the frog's energy was focused on doing what a frog does best. Isn't it interesting how a frog is actually safest when the dominant energy it is responding to is flow, not fear?

Like that frog, you need a certain amount of fear to keep you alert and safe. And like the frog, you have amazing ability at your disposal to deal with the threats that come your way when your full faculties are put to use. If you allow fear to dominate in a time of peril, real or perceived, your response actually puts you at greater risk even though you may believe that you are taking the threat more seriously. Instead of obsessing over whatever you lack to overcome the danger, it is wiser—and safer—to set aside the vast majority of your fear, then look beyond it to find your true power.

Easier said than done.

Chances are, unless you are a spiritual giant operating on levels far higher than the rest of us, you spend a great deal of your life focusing on, and fearing, your shortcomings. You worry that you don't measure up to other people's standards, or your own. You suspect that if others knew who you "really" are, they would either reject you outright or think far less of you. Perhaps a friend or two has even confirmed your fears by rejecting you after deciding that you had failed them in some way.

This same fear often carries over to God. Most people—even those who by all outward appearances are pillars of faith—quietly suspect that if God saw who they "really" are they would be deemed unworthy of God's love and attention. Many pay lip service to their undying love for God, and God's love for them, but internally they do whatever they can to avoid any possibility of a deep or intimate relationship with God that would expose their darker side. They pack churches and self-help seminars that play to their need for self-affirmation assuming that if they can just believe the affirmations the darker side will go away. Of course, it never does.

BLACK HOLE FAITH

In the Christian tradition, there is no greater waypoint in life's Dark Wood that helps us move beyond the fear of our shortcomings, and even our fear of God, than the Cross. Many people find the Cross to be a morbid symbol or one that perpetuates unhealthy notions of guilt and shame we had best move beyond in the modern world. Yet I find the opposite is true. It is a "dark" symbol to be sure, but in the Dark Wood of life, one soon discovers that darkness is not always what it appears. Treasures that many overlook are to be found in darkness.

In my experience, the Cross acts like a kind of giant black hole. Black holes in outer space are places of extreme gravitational pull that act on objects orbiting them in such a way that they draw ever closer until finally passing what is known as an *event horizon*. At the event horizon, the force of gravity is so strong that not even light can escape its grasp. Everything is drawn into the black hole's mysterious center—a point or region of infinite density known as a *singularity*. If a black hole could be compared to a giant waterfall, the event horizon would be the place where the flow toward the fall is so strong that a kayaker trying desperately to paddle upstream loses his or her ability to resist the current and succumbs to the inevitable. What happens to objects once inside a black hole is a mystery. Some believe that black holes are portals to other universes on the other side. Yet all that is really known about the inside of a black hole is that at the point of singularity all the known laws of physics break down. Like Las Vegas, what happens inside a black hole *stays* in a black hole!

The Cross of Jesus draws me to it much like a black hole, and acts on me much like reaching a singularity point. I begin to sense the gravity of the Cross when I ask myself the question that many Christians ask themselves: If I had been alive in Jesus' day, would I have crucified him? My initial reaction is, "Of course not! I'm a Christian minister, after all! I would *never* have sent Jesus to the Cross." Yet before I have even finished making this response, I can already feel the Cross's pull more strongly. I may not have stood with the angry mob before Pilate demanding that Jesus be crucified. Yet even if I was one of Jesus' closest disciples, can I really claim that I would not have participated in his crucifixion in some way? One of Jesus' innermost circle betrayed him. The rest abandoned him, or like Peter, denied knowing him in his greatest hour of need. Am I better than Peter?

More likely, if I wasn't one of Jesus' disciples, I would have been like Pilate, knowing there was something innocent, mysterious, and special about Jesus but too afraid to take a stand against the mob, believing the personal cost would be too high. If Jesus were to appear in modern times, I doubt the situation would be better. If I were not like Pilate, then I would probably be a busy, modern American instead. I'd receive word of the danger he was in and probably sympathize with his cause. I might even be enough of a "known sympathizer" to be invited to the "Justice for Jesus" support rally. Yet in the end, my calendar would be "too full" to make it. "Who is going to run the kids to soccer practice if I go? And then there's the committee meeting I'm chairing, and we're having guests to dinner, and..."

Over the course of my life, I've probably run a thousand different scenarios involving me, Jesus, and the Cross. Each one ends badly—for both of us. I find myself paddling as hard as I can against current of culpability but eventually I pass the "event horizon" of my denial. Once I admit that I'm no different from anyone else, I feel myself rapidly pulled down toward the "singularity" where all of humanity becomes one. As I plunge toward this singular place, I realize that my betrayal has not only been of Jesus but *myself*. As I consider my journey through life, I realize that over and over I have sensed the inward call of the Spirit, inviting me to follow the sweet-spot moments that mark the path of my greatest aliveness— my place in this world, my "home." Time and again I have turned aside from these moments, either too afraid of the opposition I will likely encounter, or what others might think or say. Or I have been "too busy," even too lazy. Rather than admitting any these things I have tried to deny sensing the Spirit's invitations altogether.

Finally reaching the point of "singularity" where I accept the full weight of my brokenness, it becomes clear that I have no inherent ability to find my true path in this world, or follow it, while relying on my own power, reasoning, intelligence, or even my own faithfulness or morality. If I am to experience what it is like to be fully alive before I die, I must—*must*—depend on a power far greater than myself to make the journey with me.

Just as all the known laws of physics are broken at the singularity point of a black hole, so all those who find themselves at this point of human "singularity" discover that the laws of humanity, and *theology* for that matter, are broken and transformed into something beyond our comprehension. At our place of greatest despair over ourselves and our abilities, we discover a Presence who loves us beyond our imagining, who *chooses relationship over perfection*. Life is not over. It has just begun. Like Rumi, we find ourselves in a field "out beyond the ideas of wrongdoing and right-doing." An *Unexpected Love* meets us there. And we discover that the only thing we have truly lost at the center of our inner black hole (and at the base of the Cross) is our fear.

The book of Proverbs claims "the beginning of wisdom is the fear of the LORD" (Proverbs 9:10). This may be true, but the "black hole faith" to which the Cross draws us reveals that this fear is not the sort we expect. It is not a form of terror or trepidation. In fact, the word *fear* in Proverbs is best translated "awe-struck reverence." It is this form of fear that we encounter when we lose faith in ourselves and place it in *The Unexpected Love*. How can we not stand in awe-struck reverence before a Presence who clearly sees our imperfections, our brokenness and guilt—indeed, our *emptiness*—yet chooses to be in relationship with us nonetheless? Standing in this place is the beginning of all wisdom, and all true understanding. What we thought would be the place of our greatest emptiness and fullest negation proves to be the safest and most beautiful spot in the world in which to stand.

OF THE *HUMUS*

Seen from this perspective, the Dark Wood gift of emptiness is one of the happiest gifts of all. It pushes us into a wide and sunny clearing beyond our constant calculations of "wrongdoing and rightdoing" into authentic relationship with the Holy Spirit. There we find all our imperfections are still with us, only we have lost our fear of them (in the classic sense of the word). In their place we discover a new *humility*. Like fear, however, this kind of humility is not what we expect. In the classic understanding, "humility" is about lowliness and negation of self-worth. Yet in the biblical sense, humility is about human worth and fulfillment.

The ancient Hebrews would point you to the prophet Moses as the clearest example of what true humility looks like. According to the Torah, "the man Moses was humble, more so than anyone on earth" (Numbers 12:3). Moses? Isn't Moses the one who cou-

rageously confronted Pharaoh in Egypt asking—no, *demanding*—
that Pharaoh free the Israelite slaves from bondage? Is not Moses
the one who is said to have parted the Red Sea, boldly leading,
and often goading, his people through the Sinai wilderness to the
Promised Land? Moses was no wallflower, nor was he the slightest
bit self-effacing or self-deprecating before any human being, no
matter what the person's stature. If Moses were meek or humble
according to *modern* understanding, one would expect to find him
bowing before Pharaoh asking if there's any extra work he can do.

The word *humble* comes from the Latin root, *humus,* or "earth,"
which is also at the root of "human." To be humble is to be "of the
humus" or earth. All humans are of the *humus.* Thus being humble
implies not the slightest lowliness relative to other human beings.
Someone who is of the *humus* is only lowly with respect to that
which is above the *humus:* the divine. Moses impressed the Hebrews with his humility because the only power to which he would
bow down was not Pharaoh (who was himself "of the *humus*"), but
to God.

Moses experienced a number of sweet-spot moments that convinced him that God was calling him to confront Pharaoh. Thus,
despite the odds that were clearly stacked against Moses, despite
even his own faults and shortcomings, which he was clearly aware
of and even tried to use as an excuse to be relieved of his calling
by God, Moses ultimately trusted his call, not his lack. He trusted
that whatever abilities he had been given would be enough to carry
out his calling so long as they were surrendered to God. This trust
moved Moses from fear to flow.

The fact that Moses became an immensely powerful leader and liberator of his people should not be particularly surprising. Just consider those you know who have stopped obsessing about their emptiness and uncertainty and humbly follow their sense of call in life. Are their lives more or less powerful as a result? They may not necessarily reside at the top of society's social or professional pyramid but, like Moses, they tap into the only real power that matters, and thrive there.

Of course, Forrest Church reminds us that being "of the *humus*" means that none of us is a paragon of perfection or virtue. We constantly fall short of the ideals we set for ourselves and expect of others. We miss our mark, living far from our fullest power and potential, sometimes very far, for a very long time. Yet if we are to grasp the Dark Wood gift of emptiness, we must be just as ready to claim our true power and potential as we are to concede our tendency to fall short of it. By embracing our humility—the kind we discover beyond the "singularity point" of the Cross—we live into our fullest *humanity*. We experience the paradox of encountering God's fullness within our emptiness.

ON EARTH . . .

This connection between emptiness, God, and humanity is profound. It is knit within the very structure of the human body itself. (As we will soon see, it is reflected in the heavens as well.) While there are as many different ideas about what it means to be human as there are human beings, one thing all may agree on is that to be human is to be embodied. While this fact may seem overly obvious and elementary, consider the implications of having a physical body. Could our *physicality* suggest anything about our *humanity* or our connection to God?

Your body is a finely tuned receiver of massive amounts of empirical data that internal systems convert into what might be generalized as biological and intuitive knowledge. Glance up from this book for a moment and take a look around. How many objects would you estimate are in front of you? In your living room, perhaps a hundred? Looking onto a city street, perhaps a thousand or more? Yet scientists tell us that while you were looking around, your eyes received information and sent it to your brain at the rate of roughly 10 million bits of data per second.[3] How much data is 10 million per second? The total population of Los Angeles County is just shy of 10 million.[4] If each person in the Los Angeles metropolitan area were to represent a single bit of data, your eyes and brain working together receive, process, and assimilate the equivalent of the entire population of Los Angeles *every second*.

You're not aware of all this data passing through, of course, because your brain instantaneously converts it into a coherent picture. It's quick. It's painless. It's effortless. This latter point about effortlessness is important, and we'll come around to it again shortly.

The massive data reception and conversion process undertaken by your visual cortex, in turn, generates further data in the form of thoughts and feelings. Add the data received through your sense of smell, sound, touch, and taste and you get an idea of the dizzying amounts of information your body is processing, synthesizing, condensing, and forming conclusions about. Each and every second. Without your head exploding!

Even more impressive is the fact that your body is able to detect that anything exists at all. If you hold out your hand, for instance, you see a hand. "Big deal," you say. Yet on a quantum level your hand is a very big deal. That hand is made up of billions of atoms. These atoms, in turn, contain a nucleus made of protons and neutrons and an electron cloud circling the nucleus. Even with so many atoms crammed into such a small space as your hand, the distance between the atom's nucleus and its circling electron cloud, on a relative scale, is roughly the equivalent of *the distance between the earth and the sun*. Seen from another perspective, if you set a grape seed in the center of a football stadium representing the nucleus of an atom, the perimeters of the stadium would be its electron cloud. That hand you're looking at is approximately 99.9999 percent empty space! Yet if someone hits you in the jaw, you don't say, "Gee, that would have hurt if your hand and my jaw were more than just empty space." You feel the impact and respond.

Realizing that we are all basically assemblages of vast, empty space, it seems almost inconceivable that all this empty space could be said to have something psychologists call consciousness, awareness, or mind (even "higher mind") of any kind. Or a soul.

Admittedly, the soul is hard to pin down. One of my favorite descriptions of soul that speaks to its nature and character is that of Parker Palmer, who compares the soul to a wild animal:

Like a wild animal, soul is tough, resilient, resourceful, savvy, and self-sufficient: it knows how to survive in hard places. I learned about these qualities during my bouts with depression [that is, Palmer's entry into the Dark Wood]. In that deadly darkness, the faculties I had always depended on collapsed. My intellect was useless; my emotions were dead; my will was impotent; my ego was shattered. But from time to time, deep in the thickets of my inner wilderness [that is, within the Dark Wood itself], I could sense the presence of something that knew how to stay alive even when the rest of me wanted to die. That something was my tough and tenacious soul.

Yet despite its toughness, the soul is also shy. Just like a wild animal, it seeks safety in the dense underbrush, especially when other people are around. If we want to see a wild animal, we know that the last thing we should do is go crashing through the woods yelling for it to come out. But if we will walk quietly into the woods, sit patiently at the base of a tree, breathe with the earth, and fade into our surroundings, the wild creature we seek might put in an appearance. We may see it only briefly and only out of the corner of an eye—but the sight is a gift we will always treasure as an end in itself.[5]

As Palmer's experience of depression suggests, many of us enter the Dark Wood during a "dark night of the soul." But the Dark Wood is not depression. Depression may simply serve as an entry point, as it did for Palmer. The Dark Wood, in Palmer's experience, was a beautiful, mysterious place where he discovered a wild and powerful presence within himself (soul), which was itself connected to an even more wild, powerful presence (God's Spirit).

Is it not rather amazing what goes on within such a vast amount of empty space known as the human body? We literally embody the message that within great emptiness resides great fullness.

. . . AS IT IS IN HEAVEN

A similar message is repeated in the heavens above us. A couple summers ago I spent a few weeks at my family's cabin on the Oregon Coast south of Bandon. I had arrived a week ahead of my family to spend some time alone to write. On the seventh day of my writing retreat, I shut my laptop down around midnight and went to bed. At 3:00 a.m. I was awakened with a jolt by the sound of my wife, Melanie, calling insistently, "Eric!" I sat straight up, searched for her beside me, and realized I'd been dreaming. Melanie was still back in Omaha.

After I wiped the sand from my eyes, my vision came into focus on a reddish orb glowing faintly in the night sky outside my bedroom window. This was the same dot of light that Melanie and I had stared at for years while standing on the lakeshore of this very cabin during family vacations. We had always assumed it was Mars. But now, gazing at it from its 3:00 a.m. position, doubt slowly crept in.

Sleepily, I reached for my iPhone, pressing the home button firmly. A soft glow filled my face as the phone awakened from its own slumber. Brushing through two screens of applications, I found Star Walk and opened it.

Holding the phone toward the window, a map quickly materialized, showing the entire night sky directly in front of me. Dead center was the red orb that had ignited my curiosity. Touching my finger to it locked the screen in place and a target appeared over the red orb. Double clicking magnified the screen several times, revealing that what I was looking at was not in fact Mars, but Star HR 7790, of the constellation Pavo.

Hitting the info button filled half the screen with an image of HR 7790, the other half with its astronomical biography. According to Star Walk, HR 7790 is also known as "Peacock":

> [The name Peacock] was assigned to the star by Her Majesty's Nautical Almanac Office in the late 1930s during the creation of The Air Almanac, a navigational almanac for the Royal Air Force. Of the fifty-seven stars included in the new almanac, two had no classical names.... The RAF insisted that all of the stars must have names, so new names were invented. Alpha Pavonis was named Peacock.

What really stood out was Peacock's distance from earth: 178.8 light years. Of course, compared to other stars, Peacock is practically a next-door neighbor. Yet, lying back down in bed that night, I started doing some mental math. "Let's see, light travels at 186,000 miles per second. I wonder how many seconds there are in a year?" A quick Google search on the iPhone revealed the answer: 31,556,926. I punched these numbers into the phone's calculator to figure the mileage between Peacock and Earth: 31,556,926 x 186,000 x 178.8. The answer came back with 15 zeros!

I thought to myself, *How is it that I, a mere mortal, can be aware of an object over a thousand trillion miles away? I have a hard enough time remembering where I've placed my glasses!*

That thought brought me back to a worship service I once led in which we poured out a sixteen-ounce can of Morton Salt while walking down the center aisle toward the Communion table. As the stream of salt poured onto the carpet we noted that the Milky Way Galaxy in which we make our home is 100,000 light years in diameter and, on average, 1,000 light years thick. What a vast amount of empty space! Yet astronomers currently estimate that our galaxy contains approximately 200 billion stars, most of which are quite a bit larger than our sun. (You could fit a million earths inside our sun.) As salt continued to stream from the can, we invited the congregation to envision each grain of salt representing a single star of the Milky Way. When we reached the Communion table, the salt finally finished pouring and we informed the congregation that in order to represent all the stars in our galaxy alone it would take over 76,000 cans of Morton Salt!

A thought surfaced from the deep recesses of my imagination, almost as if it had been whispered in my ear: *If we mere mortals are aware of the existence of all these things which are so incomprehensibly far away, imagine what God's consciousness must be like!*

Seen from one angle, technology has increased our awareness of the size of the universe so greatly that for the first time in human history, many openly wonder how God could possibly be aware of us, if God exists at all. Yet seen from another angle, the same scientific advancements have made us more aware than ever before just how far even our limited human consciousness extends. Could science be inviting us to conceive anew of the possibility of God's conscious awareness of us? Not everyone would answer the same way. But what can be said with certainty is that when we look to the stars in the night sky we get the same message as when we look to the atoms of our hands: within great emptiness resides great fullness!

For Christians, one of the greatest symbols of the Dark Wood gift of emptiness is the Cross. Here we find the emptiness of the heavens merging with the emptiness of a human body. At their intersection we hear the emptiest and most human of all cries on the lips of Jesus, "My God, my God, why have you forsaken me?" In that great and terrible moment of emptiness, not even Jesus could find God. Yet for the last two thousand years, Christians have insisted that the Cross is not the end of the story, but the beginning of a new one. Why? Not because Jesus found God as he stared from the Cross into the vast emptiness of the heavens, but because from within this Great Emptiness *God found Jesus*. The message could not be more profound: If you yearn to find God, get empty! Let God *find you*.

WHERE THE RUBBER HITS THE ROAD

A good friend of mine named Bruce Van Blair found it hard to sleep one night a number of years ago. He simply could not stop thinking of a friend he had neither seen nor heard from in months who lived two hours away. Something nagged at him in a way that suggested that his friend was in deep trouble. Every attempt at sleep backfired, and he'd find himself sitting up in bed thinking about his friend. Finally, around 1:30 in the morning, he sheepishly awakened his wife and told her he needed to visit his friend. Naturally, she thought he'd gone crazy. For that matter, so did Bruce! But he got in his car and drove out into the night. Arriving at his friend's doorstep at 3:30 a.m., Bruce felt awkward and foolish: "This is insane! He's never going to think of you as rational again. You don't even know if he's home!"

Gathering his courage, Bruce knocked at the door. No answer. He knocked a little louder. Still no answer. Figuring his friend might be deep in sleep, he knocked a third time more loudly. He could hear footsteps approaching. The porch light came on. After a brief pause, the door opened, revealing his friend looking more than a little bewildered. "Bruce?!"

Bruce entered his friend's house, explaining what had brought him there. His friend looked no less bewildered, saying, "Thanks, but I'm fine." They sat and drank coffee for over an hour. They had both moved from Paxton, Massachusetts, about the same time and had not seen or spoken to each other since the move. At last, Bruce rose and left. If Bruce had a tail, it would have been solidly between his legs as he returned home, frustrated that he'd been so impulsive. He tried to put the thought out of his mind.

Three months later, Bruce's friend was driving down from Maine and stopped by his house in Andover, Massachusetts, for an unexpected visit. He had come to tell Bruce that he hadn't been honest with him the night Bruce showed up on his doorstep. He had been awake when Bruce knocked. Wide awake.

"I was sitting in the dining room in the dark with a loaded revolver in my hand."

What Bruce's friend said next he has never forgotten: "You didn't have to say a word. I knew only one power in the universe could have brought you to my door at that particular moment. I had drifted far from God, but in that moment I knew God still cared about me. So I decided I better hang around a little longer to see what God wanted me to do."

Bruce's experience reminds me that the soul is so elusive and untamable partly because it is connected to a larger story. The Holy Spirit frequently throws us intuitions that come from a source completely beyond ourselves. Often these intuitions or gut instincts seem confusing. They are connected to a part of our story that we can't directly reach. Sometimes the connection seems even to transcend time and space. Yet we recognize that it's our soul responding to Spirit when the intuition, though strange or unexpected ("Go visit your friend who lives two hours away in the middle of the night"), hits us precisely where we live. We experience it as a sweet-spot moment—often a series of them—where something deep within seems to click into place and cry "Home!" The empty space within us charges with fullness and our soul, like a rubber ball submerged beneath the water, strains against whatever is set in its way until released into freedom. We move from fear to flow, discovering a power at work within and beyond us that is far greater than we are, yet is intimately connected to us as well. We discover what it means to be fully human.

4

THE GIFT OF BEING THUNDERSTRUCK

If a man wishes to be sure of the road he treads on,
he must close his eyes and walk in the dark.
—Saint John of the Cross

THE NEXT GIFT TO BE FOUND in the Dark Wood, the gift of being thunderstruck, was widely recognized by the ancients, but is perhaps the least understood in modern times. Some consider ancient ways of understanding to be primitive or superstitious. Yet many ancient cultures developed a surprisingly advanced vocabulary for describing patterns they observed both in the external and internal world that have been lost to us. If we observe how the ancients spoke of lightning and thunder, it becomes more apparent how their mythological imagination helped them negotiate life's path.

The power of mythological imagination lies not in its ability to describe historical events that took place in the distant past but to identify contours of human behavior and experience that are encountered repeatedly throughout history on down to our own day.

Myths and stories create a map of the "world within the world"—the invisible geography that humanity may use to avoid life's dead ends and lead it to a place of freedom. Because the geography is not visible to the naked eye, traversing it is always a bit like journeying into the darkness. Hence, the ancient metaphor of the Dark Wood. The Dark Wood is that inner terrain you negotiate more through intuition, imagination, and indirect ways of knowing than through direct perception.

In every mythology in the Ancient Near East, the elements of lightning and thunder are depicted in similar fashion: as instruments for conveying the voice of the highest deity. The imagery is the same whether one is examining the monotheistic, Yahweh-worshiping culture of ancient Israel or the polytheistic, Marduk-worshiping culture of Mesopotamia. It is the same for Zeus among the Greeks, Tahundi and Ivriz among the Anatolian cultures, and Baal among the Canaanites. In their artistic representations as well as their literature, each of these cultures envisions their most high (or only) deity speaking to us most centrally through lightning and thunder.

Here is one of many examples from the Hebrew Scriptures:

> *Listen, listen to the* thunder *of [God's] voice*
>   *and the* rumbling *that comes from his mouth.*
> *Under the whole heaven he lets it loose,*
>   *and his* lightning *to the corners of the earth.*
> *After it his voice* roars;
>   *he* thunders *with his majestic voice*

and he does not restrain the lightnings *when his*
voice is heard.
God thunders *wondrously with his voice;*
    he does great things that we cannot comprehend.
(Job 37:2-5 NRSV, emphasis added)

Why are thunder and lightning so commonly depicted as conveying the voice of the divine? The conventional assumption has long been that "primitive" cultures invented such myths to explain the origin of storms. This assumption is more the product of modern scientific imagination than mythological imagination. The purpose was not to explain where lightning and thunder come from but to explain where the *voice of God* comes from, and more important, how it comes *to us* through intuition.

Have you ever experienced a sudden flash of insight or awareness that rocked your whole world? Perhaps you experienced a sudden flash when you encountered your first love or life partner, or when a child was born, or perhaps you went out for a casual walk in the woods one day, only to return a different person. Why do we describe these moments as "sudden flashes" or "seeing the light" when there is nothing to see? Why do we claim that they "rock" our world when the actual world around us remains stable? Like the ancients we, too, are forced to convey interior phenomena using concrete, external metaphors. What the ancients were trying to describe, which we moderns are too "sophisticated" to realize, is how the divine speaks to us. When the ancients spoke of the deity flashing lightning and chasing it with claps of thunder, they meant that the voice of the divine often comes through momentary flashes of intuition or awareness that trigger sensations that reverberate within us like rolling thunder.

Over the course of my career, people have asked me repeatedly why God doesn't speak to people "like in the Bible" anymore. Yet, everyone with whom I've conversed for more than a few minutes has spoken of times when "the lightbulb came on," or they had an "aha" moment or "moment of clarity" when something "clicked into place" that impacted their life's direction in some way. "So," I say, "how are you so sure that God doesn't still speak 'like in the Bible' anymore?"

While you may be able to identify times when you've experienced flashes of insight, you may find the thunder easier to locate. In an actual storm you may miss the lightning entirely. It is brief, soundless, and often comes from a distant place. But even quiet thunder is hard to miss. Even if you overlook or forget the inner realization that triggers your inner thunder, the ongoing reverberations caused by the lightning sometimes last for years. I cannot remember the specific moment when I first realized that I wanted to marry Melanie, for instance, but the reverberations have continued to thunder for twenty-six years.

The fact of the matter is that God never speaks with an audible voice in the Bible, just as God does not do this in our day. While the Bible is full of God-talk, its authors were trying to convey what was "heard" internally when the lightning hit. They reflected upon the implications of that flash of insight, or moment of clarity, or "aha" experience sometimes for months or years, later recording these implications with the preface, "And God said…" They weren't being dishonest. The ancients simply did not envision a time when the mythological imagination would be such a distant memory that people would take the metaphor literally!

Of course, those who recorded what they considered to be their high god's words were as flawed as we are. They were perfectly capable of misinterpreting the significance of these flashes of awareness or their implications. Yet they did not misinterpret how the voice of the divine comes to us. Nearly every religion and culture on earth has its way of stating that one of the best ways to hear the voice of the divine is to pay attention to the "lightning and thunder."

In the Dark Wood of our interior journey, when the lightning flashes and thunder reverberates powerfully and repeatedly in the same location, it is a good sign that we are to move in the direction it indicates. We feel drawn to move in this direction because it calls to our deepest self and feels most natural. In the film *Adaptation*, based on Susan Orlean's book *The Orchid Thief*, an unorthodox orchid hunter named John Laroche reminds us of what it's like to sense the call when he speaks of the attraction between a bee and the specific orchid it is meant to pollinate:

> There's a certain orchid that looks exactly like a certain insect so the insect is drawn to this flower—its double, its soul mate—and wants nothing more than to make love to it. After the insect flies off, it spots another soul-mate flower and makes love to it, thus pollinating it. And neither

flower nor the insect will ever understand the significance of their lovemaking. I mean, how could they know that because of their little dance the world lives, but it does. By simply doing what they're designed to do, something large and magnificent happens. In this sense they show us how to live, how the only barometer you have is your heart; how when you spot your flower you can't let anything get in your way.[1]

THIRTY FRENCH BALLERINAS

Perhaps we're all more closely related to the bees and other animals than we realize. When a bee is drawn to its orchid, its body produces hormones and electro-chemical signals that tell the bee that it is heading toward the right orchid. Similarly, moving in the direction to which the lightning and thunder calls us tends to produce sensations that are not only inward and spiritual but concrete and physical as well. The human body responds hormonally, electrically, and chemically when we take a step in the right direction. If you pay careful attention to your body, you may notice a sensation akin to letting go of something that you have been grasping too tightly. You may notice your breathing grow more relaxed and easy in response to a certain thought. Some people experience a warming sensation in their abdomen or quiet sense of well-being arising within them. However your body responds, it will normally feel like something has clicked into place that triggers a sensation of inner peace or joy, even if that sensation is quite subtle and even if the direction toward which you feel called appears difficult. These are what we have been calling sweet-spot moments.

Admittedly, eating Cheetos can produce similar sensations. Chemistry is chemistry. The foods we crave attract us because they trigger a chemical release inside our bodies that produces feelings of happiness, satiation, and well-being. Mass producers of processed foods are well aware of body chemistry and have specifically designed products that produce feelings of health and wholeness even when the product itself is unhealthy and devoid of nutritional value. Thus, we must always ask ourselves a question I once heard author Phyllis Tickle ask: "Was that the Holy Spirit talking or the pizza I just ate?"[2]

Temporarily, the foods we eat and other external stimuli can produce feelings that are similar to those we feel when having an authentic spiritual experience. Why do you think a spiritually starved society struggles so much with obesity and obsession with sex? One of the hallmarks of authentic spiritual experience, however, is that it continues to repeat itself—like thunder and lightning in a good storm—long after the pizza is gone.

Incidentally, this is why I rarely trust leaps of faith. In my profession, I encounter people regularly who have hit dead ends and even stumbled into significant danger by taking what they call "a leap of faith." They suddenly marry someone, or move across the country, or quit a job in response to a fleeting sensation of well-being that they associate with God or the universe commanding them to leap off some figurative cliff and fly. When the sensation goes away and (appropriate) doubt creeps in, they associate this doubt with backsliding or failing to "trust the revelation." Having leapt and discovered that the air beneath their feet was too thin to support their weight, they come into my office feeling hurt and betrayed by God or the universe, vowing never to listen for the divine again.

We've all made this mistake in one way or another. Yet we must realize that leaps of faith are the junk food of the spiritual realm. While it is true that the Holy Spirit does, at times, invite you to take a leap into the Great Unknown (or plunge into our elemental waters like Rilke's swan), the Spirit rarely does so without leading you to the edge of the cliff by way of a thousand smaller steps. By the time you reach the edge, therefore, you have responded to so many sweet-spot moments and experienced so much confirmation of your direction that the leap isn't so much a leap but one more small step. An authentic leap of faith may become the first step of a new beginning, but taking that step feels more like the culmination of a long and engaging journey.

One way I often describe what it is like to sense and follow the Spirit's direction is that it feels like the sound of *thirty French ballerinas talking.* In the winter of 1985, I visited the French village of Chinon along the Loire River en route to Nantes where I would study for the spring term. On a student's budget, I avoided Chinon's costly hotels by staying the night at a youth hostel connected to an athletic facility—the French version of a YMCA. My room was adjacent to the gymnasium.

The following morning I was awakened by a sound that, to this day, I consider the most beautiful I have ever heard. Just before waking, I had an unusual dream. I dreamt that I was standing in the Jewish Temple of the prophet Isaiah's vision, in which he beheld God enthroned in the Holy of Holies, smoke filling the air, and winged beings known as seraphim flying around the throne singing, "Holy, holy, holy!" (Isaiah 6). I stood there captivated by the unimaginable beauty of their singing. What was provoking this dream was the sound of thirty young French girls jabbering excitedly in the hallway outside my room. While the voices of children in every culture are beautiful, the jibber-jabber of excited *French* children is especially infectious. They half-speak, half-sing to their peers. I call it the sound of "liquid joy." While I was ill-prepared to translate what I heard into words (my last grade in college French had been a C+), the essence of what they were saying was clear: "We're about to do something *extremely exciting*! We can *hardly wait*!"

Half asleep but fully entranced, I rose from my bed, unlatched the door, and stepped into the hallway to behold the girls, whom I estimated to be between the ages of four and six, all festooned in blazing red tutus. Immediately, I was brought back to my senses as one of their number burst out laughing, pointed at me, and blurted, "*Ooh la la! Regardez son peejays!*" ("Oh my! Look at his pajamas!"). The ballerinas giggled hysterically as I shrank behind the door, latching it quickly and bracing myself against it, embarrassed by my lack of discretion.

Back in bed, the heavenly cacophony continued. It transported me, now fully awake, to a most holy place. Chances are, you know this place quite well, or are at least familiar with it, even if you've never experienced the "liquid joy" of thirty French ballerinas. Amidst the thousand voices that chatter within you, there is one voice that comes from a place that is perfectly safe, perfectly free from anxiety. It is not reacting to, or running from, anything. In this place you experience no sense of judgment or condemnation—by your peers, by your conscience, or by God. The voice that speaks from this place knows what's most important to you, and for you. It is the voice of your deepest freedom, your truest self. Often when I'm privileged enough to overhear this deep, inner voice I discover that what it considers important is quite different from what I consider important on more superficial levels where I am beset by anxiety, anger, or fear. In this small but very real place— this Holy of Holies—the questions, yearnings, hopes, and dreams that well up within me are most closely aligned with my particular calling.

Back in the hostel, the sound of those French ballerinas had put me so completely into this place that I was literally dreaming about the Holy of Holies! After awakening, embarrassing myself, and lying back down, I remained in this precious internal space. There, I found my thoughts drifting from my hallway embarrassment back to a subject that had been afflicting me since my first night in Europe. Three weeks earlier I had landed in London and, that first evening, found myself engrossed in a two-hour conversation with a New Zealander I met in a pizza restaurant. When the meal was over, the gentleman picked up the bill, looked me straight in the eye and said, "You'll be going to seminary after you graduate. I'm sure of it."

"How on earth can you know that?" I exclaimed in utter shock. While the subject of ministry had arisen in our conversation, I had offered such a long list of reasons why the ministry was the *last* vocation I wanted to enter that it seemed almost insulting that my dinner companion would make such a prediction. Had he listened to *anything* I'd said?

"Listen," he assured me, "I'm so convinced you're going to be a minister that the only thing I ask in exchange for buying your dinner tonight is that you send me an invitation to your ordination."

"Thank you," I replied, "but don't wear yourself out walking to the mailbox and back."

That morning in the Chinon hostel, while exploring the interior space opened wide by the ballerinas' liquid joy, I found myself imagining going to seminary and becoming a minister—and *enjoying* the vision. I did not recoil in fear at the image of myself as a minster as I had over dinner three weeks earlier, nor did I seek to cast the vision aside as I had for three solid years since it first came to me. In those days, I considered ministers to be almost universally crazy and probably a bit sadomasochistic (I'm still not sure that I wasn't right!). During my senior year of high school when the thought first occurred, I had deliberately set a course to steer myself as far away from the ministry as I could get, enrolling in a secular college and declaring a major in economics. Yet, inside the Holy of Holies where I could overhear the voice of my True Self, the joy within that voice was the same as the joy being transmitted by those French ballerinas. The ballerinas had found their orchid and I had found mine.

I would lose this feeling of liquid joy many times before finally sending the New Zealander an invitation to my ordination ten years later, after receiving both a master's of Divinity and a doctorate in Biblical Studies. But every time I would lose it, it would circle back again, with growing intensity. Each time it returned, it produced the same mental and physical sensations I'd experienced when enraptured in that Chinon hostel. To this day, I continue to pay close attention to whatever thoughts are in my mind at the moment I experience these sweet-spot moments. They act like crumbs in the Dark Wood of life that indicate the direction of my particular path ahead. I have learned that I can trust these moments when they keep returning and pointing in a similar direction.

NONIHC

It would be a mistake to conclude from these observations about my path to ministry that only ministers and workers in "spiritual" professions feel a sense of calling in life, or that the only people who find and live into their place in this world are people of faith. All of us have a meaning and purpose to our lives, a calling that is unique to us and brings us fully alive. While working on a draft of this book, I spent more time at our family cabin on the southern Oregon coast where I had my encounter with the Peacock Star. One day I was lured away from my work by my brother-in-law, Paul, a local resident and fellow foodie. The city of Roseburg, ninety minutes away, was hosting the band Pink Martini for a concert series beside the Umpqua River. As enticing as the Afro-Cuban rhythms and sumptuous salsa music served up by Pink Martini sounded, what sealed the deal was Paul's suggestion that we leave a few hours early to taste the velvety Pinot Noirs, Syrahs, and Temprenillos for which the Umpqua Valley is being increasingly recognized. We could visit the wineries in the afternoon, and bring a bottle to the concert to sip beside the river along with some hors d'oeuvres. How could I resist?

We picked up another foodie friend named Dove and set off for the Umpqua Valley. As we made our way, Paul told us of a wine maker from Hillcrest Winery who had impressed him with his enthusiasm for the craft and his encyclopedic knowledge of wines from around the world. I'd tasted a sip or two of Hillcrest wine previously and had already put the winery on the top of my list of visits. Now, I was even more anxious to arrive in the Umpqua.

Being the northernmost winery on our itinerary, Hillcrest would be the last vineyard on our afternoon tour. As we journeyed from tasting room to tasting room, we were careful not to linger too long lest Hillcrest close before we arrived. Adding to our urgency was the fact that Hillcrest doesn't sell its wine in stores. With a limited production of just 1,400 cases, the fruits of Hillcrest's labors are sold to only a handful of restaurants—and people who visit the winery.

Despite our careful planning, we arrived at Hillcrest five minutes *after* closing time. But finding the tasting room door unlocked, we slipped inside and managed to coax Hillcrest's owner and winemaker, Dyson DeMara, into uncorking the wines he'd just put away. It wasn't difficult.

"I'm happy to pour a couple of tastes but unfortunately I've got a commitment I've got to get to," Dyson stated apologetically, "so I won't be able to spend much time with you."

As we sipped one incredible wine after another, Dyson became increasingly animated. While none of us were wine experts, apparently Dyson was happy to be in the company of people who could at least tell the difference between a Syrah and a Semillon. Dyson told us the history of each wine—not only its heritage at Hillcrest, but its historical roots and stylistic variances in Italy, France, Portugal, Spain, and Hungary. As he talked, Dyson radiated the quiet joy of someone who is completely in love with what he does. The sound of thirty French ballerinas was in his voice!

A half hour later, I knew we'd stayed well beyond the point when Dyson needed to leave, so I suggested we drink up and let him be. "Oh no, this is my joy, my art, I'm happy to stay a little longer. You know, I've got a new wine I just put in the bottles. It's not quite ready for serving, but if you use a little imagination, you'll be able to tell where it's headed."

Dyson disappeared briefly into a back room and reappeared proudly bearing a bottle called "Le Pig" with a butcher's drawing of a pig sectioned into parts on the label. "Pork is my favorite meat. I wanted to create a wine that would go perfectly with pork." Thus commenced a lengthy conversation on the finer attributes of pork, Le Pig, and other meat-and-wine pairings.

In the midst of our conversation, I asked Dyson why he doesn't sell his wines in stores. "I spent years as a winemaker in the Napa Valley, working for one of the largest wineries and got burned out. I was tired of what selling to stores involves."

"What's that?" I asked.

"Endless distributor dinners and creating wines to follow whatever hot trend the public is chasing. I don't mind doing a winemaker dinner now and again, but what I really want to spend my time on is making wine." Dyson wanted to choose the varieties and develop them in the way that the grape's distinctive character-istics and heritage told him they should be done, not the market. He realized he would never have a chance to do this while working for a large commercial winery and that there was an opportunity to do it in Oregon. So he left a high-paying job with plenty of pres-tige and decided to make a go of it in the Umpqua Valley with his own little winery.

It may have been burnout that prompted Dyson's journey into Dark Wood to face the uncertainties of leaving a job and regular paycheck behind, but burnout is not what keeps him there. It's joy. All it takes is five minutes of conversation with Dyson to realize you are with someone who embodies what Confucius meant when he said, "Choose a job you love and you will never have to work another day in your life." Doubtless, Dyson works very hard, facing the enormous struggles and uncertainties of being a small busi-ness owner, laboring in his vineyards, and engaging in the tricky chemistry of fermenting raw grape juice into fine wine. Yet be-cause every ounce of effort is oriented toward doing what he loves to do, it doesn't feel like work. It often feels like play. When you find a vocation that connects you more deeply with your place in the world, you don't suddenly step out of the Dark Wood one day exclaiming, "Now I can finally live my life." Instead, you discover that the struggles and uncertainties associated with life in the Dark Wood remain. Only now, they become deeply connected to a path that brings you alive. They begin to work for you, not against you. They also begin blessing others—even the world itself.

As our conversation at Hillcrest continued, it became clear that while winemaking is central to Dyson's sense of place in this world, it is also much more than this. Rarely does a calling only involve something we do, though it does always prompt us to do something. Dyson's passion for making fine wine informs his environmental sensibilities, his sense of fairness and economic justice for those who help him make wine, his love of family, and his desire to help others develop winemaking into a high art. Winemaking at Hillcrest is a family affair in which every member of the DeMara household plays a role. Hillcrest's grapes are cultivated following sustainable, environmentally friendly processes, even though these processes produce smaller yields and less potential profit. Hillcrest's hired workers are paid fairly and are treated with the respect he gives his own family. And Dyson is always ready to find a kindred spirit in his tasting room with whom he can trade stories of wine, culture, history, and art.

The highlight of our tasting that afternoon was a wine curiously named NONIHC. NONIHC is a luscious Cabernet Franc brimming with signature blackberry and raspberry flavors, with hints of spice and tobacco brought together by silky, structured tannins, suggesting it will only get better with age. (OK, I'll admit that I read that in a wine review.) Between sips, Dyson explained that Cabernet Franc is the dominant grape in wines from a place dear to my heart—Chinon—where I heard the ballerinas! His version was meant to bring the Chinon winemaking tradition alive in the Umpqua. Suddenly the quirky name made sense. NONIHC is CHINON spelled backwards.

I have seen a similar combination of passion, joy, justice, and art reflected in many others whose professions aren't typically considered spiritual, but whose vocations take them on a deeply spiritual path. I'm reminded of two brothers for whom fixing automobiles is a key part of their calling. They get the job done right the first time and charge a fair price for their labor. The brothers never recommend work that doesn't need to be done, and you are treated so well when you visit their shop that you almost want your car to be sick just to experience the vibe of the place. Once, a friend asked one of the brothers what motivated them to do so well and be so honest. He responded, "My brother and I are Muslim. We treat *every* automobile as if Muhammad himself will be driving away in it."

A stockbroker I know takes a similar attitude, treating each client as if Jesus himself is the investor. Her conviction not only inspires her to work tirelessly to maximize her clients' investments, but also to take into account the ethics of the companies in which she invests ("Would Jesus want me investing in X, Y, or Z?"). She is also politically active, working to promote justice, particularly for the poor, in the very economic system in which she does business ("Would Jesus want money being made on the backs of the poor?").

To be sure, the Muslim auto mechanics and Christian stockbroker both follow a different set of creeds. And I have no idea what Dyson's religious background is, or if he considers himself a person of faith. What is clear, however, is that each of these professionals has been struck by lightning; that the thunder continues to reverberate strongly both in their craft and in their sense of personhood; and that doing what brings them personally alive in this world has become a channel for loving their neighbor as themselves. While each may not articulate it the same way, I believe that each person's sense of call has become a channel for loving and serving God as well.

Does this mean that faith and creeds do not matter? Not at all. It simply means that none of these individuals needs a creed to validate their place in this world. Each is responding to an inner sense of love, joy, humility, and service to which the best creeds endeavor to point. Their creed is written not on paper but in flesh and blood, in grape vines and fermentation vats, in oil pans and carburetors, in investment portfolios and voting ballots. By following a path that brings them into their fullest humanity, their lives betray the telltale marks of being touched by divinity.

5

THE GIFT OF GETTING LOST

Winning does not tempt that man. This is how he grows:
by being defeated, decisively,
by greater and greater beings.
—Rainer Maria Rilke (1875–1926)

WHEN DYSON DEMARA REALIZED that he needed to step away from a prized job working for a large Napa Valley winery in order to devote himself more fully to doing what brings him alive in this world, his awareness came as a result of feeling lost within outward success. When David Whyte realized he must commit himself wholeheartedly to the art of poetry, his awakening came as a result of feeling lost in his work at a nonprofit he strongly believed in. People who find and live into their calling rarely do so without getting lost first. Yet since there are no straight or clear paths in the Dark Wood of life, they do not cease to get lost after once being found. Rather, those who embrace life in the Dark Wood gradually learn that the regular experience of getting lost is one of the most important gifts we can receive.

The last time I visited the family cabin in Oregon, my flight took me from my home in Omaha, Nebraska, to Phoenix, Arizona. In Phoenix, I stayed on the plane for the next segment of its route, which took me to San Jose, California. In San Jose, I changed planes and flew to Portland, Oregon. Once in Portland, I rented a car and drove to Bandon. While I can't say that I much enjoyed the long day of travel, neither did my circuitous route trigger panic attacks. I was perfectly calm about the zigzags, changes of planes, and changes in modes of transportation because I knew there is no direct flight from Omaha to Bandon and because the flights were all clearly printed on my itinerary and my car rental was secured.

Our journey through life is never a straight one, even if we are paying attention to our sweet-spot moments. The path zigzags. Sometimes it heads in the exact opposite direction we think it should (like flying south toward Phoenix when Bandon lies to the northeast). Sometimes we have to "change planes" to get where we need to go (as I needed to do in San Jose). Other times we need to stay on the same "plane" and trust that it will eventually move us in a new direction (as when I stayed aboard the plane to Phoenix, which then took me to San Jose). Sometimes we need to get off the "plane" entirely and change modes of transportation (like driving from Portland to Bandon). We would probably be fine with all these twists and turns, more or less, if someone issued us a printed itinerary. But God seems to have forgotten about the itinerary.

Instead, at each point where the journey needs to make a turn we start to feel increasingly lost.

In my own journey, this feeling of being lost prompts me to pay more careful attention to the signals that the Holy Spirit sends me. I pray and meditate longer and with greater attention. I pay more attention to my gut intuitions and bodily responses. I apply the gifts of reason and logic more carefully, even while trusting that sometimes the right direction is indicated in ways that defy reason and logic. I seek the council of friends and mentors. At some point, the lightning starts flashing and the thunder starts crashing, revealing a particular way forward and confirming that I can trust the direction. I don't always get it right. Sometimes I have to reassess or backtrack and do the whole process over again until I make the next right step. But the point is, even though I get it wrong sometimes, I would be completely off course in the zigzag path of life if I didn't experience regular periods of feeling lost that alert me to pay attention.

In his poem, "Lost," David Wagoner eloquently describes what to do when you find yourself lost:

> *Stand still. The trees ahead*
> *and bushes beside you*
> *Are not lost. Wherever you are is called Here.*
> *And you must treat it as a powerful stranger.*
> *Must ask permission to know it and be known.*
> *The forest breathes. Listen. It answers.*
> *I have made this place around you.*

If you leave it you may come back again.
saying Here.
No two trees are the same to Raven.
No two branches are the same to Wren.
If what a tree or a bush does is lost on you.
You are surely lost. Stand still.
The forest knows
Where you are. You must let it find you.[1]

BRUCE ALMIGHTY

In the film *Bruce Almighty*, the protagonist, Bruce, finds himself on the edge of such a Dark Wood, though he has obviously never read David Wagoner. Bruce is far from his place in the world and feeling desperate for a sign that his life has meaning and purpose after being fired from his job as a television weatherman. As he drives down the highway one night he anxiously prays, "OK, God, you want me to talk to you? Then talk back. Tell me what's going on. What should I do? Give me a signal." Just then he passes a road construction sign flashing the words, "Caution Ahead." Oblivious to its message, he continues to pray, "I need your guidance, Lord, *please* send me a sign!" A truck full of construction signs suddenly pulls in front of him, full of warning signs like "Stop" and "Wrong Way." Exasperated, Bruce exclaims, "Ah, what's this joker doing now?" Stomping on the accelerator, swerving dangerously around the truck, he glances at his rearview mirror, noticing a set of prayer beads hung there. "OK," he says, "I'll do it your way" as he takes the beads in his hand, holds them in a tight fist, and prays, "All right. Lord, I need a miracle.... I'm desperate. I need your help, Lord. Please, reach into my life."

Suddenly, Bruce's car hits a pothole that jolts the beads out of his hand. Taking his eyes off the road, he searches and finds the beads on the floor. Clutching them triumphantly in his hands, he looks at the beads and laughs in an I'll-show-*you*-who's-boss kind of way, then looks ahead just as his car smashes into a light pole next to a lake. Stumbling out of the car, he tosses his prayer beads into the lake shouting, "Fine. The gloves are off, pal! Let me see a little wrath. Smite me, O mighty Smiter! *You're* the one who should be fired! The only one around here who's not doing his job is *you*! *Answer me!*"

Just then Bruce's pager rings. Slowly, he takes the pager off its holster and checks the number. Little does he know but it's God paging him. "Sorry. Don't know ya," he sighs. "Wouldn't call ya if I did."[2]

While it would be a mistake to believe that God calls to us in such obvious and direct ways, defying natural law with such flair, it is equally a mistake to assume that God makes no response to the plea of a soul searching for home. Frankly, I would find this little scene a lot funnier if it didn't represent the real pain and desperation of countless people who feel lost in the dark—or the extent to which any of us overlook the signals God sends.

Over the years, many have sat in a chair across from me, confessing that they don't believe God cares about them, only to recount a whole series of incidents and "coincidences" that have happened lately that all point in the direction of the Spirit's quiet and consistent response. A single mother tells me she's been asking for God's help in the midst of a financial crisis and has grown discouraged by God's apparent silence. Digging into the story more deeply, she acknowledges that yes, she did get asked to interview for a job she'd been hoping for, and yes, her ex-husband suddenly sent a child support check after three years of sending nothing (shame on the husband, but how strange the timing). She also recently figured out that she could save nearly $100 a month by cutting out cigarettes. Oh, and her five-year-old surprised her just this morning by wrapping his arms around her, telling her how dearly he loves her, and giving her a kiss on the cheek. "He *never* does that," she says. Indeed.

It is impossible to say with certainty that the Holy Spirit was behind any of these incidents, of course. Each can be explained through entirely natural causes without positing supernatural intervention. But who says that the Spirit must act supernaturally when coming to the aid of someone lost in the Dark Wood? If God is ultimately responsible for creating the natural laws by which the universe works, being content to form stars, planets, plants, and animals over 15 billion years of evolution rather than wave a magic wand and zap them into existence, then why would God be so quick to break these laws just because someone is suffering a financial setback? While "freaky" things that can't be explained through natural causes do seem to happen now and again, this probably reveals more about how little we actually know about nature than how much we know about God's supernatural intervention.

Yet the fact that God prefers natural law to supernatural intervention tells us more about *how God acts* in our world than about how God fails to act. In the words of Psalm 42, "Deep calls to deep" (v. 7 NRSV). The principle way God offers direction to someone in need while respecting freewill and the constraints of natural law is through gentle intuitions that arise within human consciousness, producing sweet-spot moments that a person is free to either accept or reject.

Applied to the situation of the mother in my office, I would not expect checks to magically appear in the mail and bank account balances to inexplicably jump higher. Rather, I would expect the Spirit to be flashing and thundering, making subtle suggestions both to the woman and to those most directly connected with her. Thus, I would advise her to be more highly attentive and watchful than usual—and willing to receive the Spirit's help.

I might expect, for instance, for the woman to feel more powerfully drawn to applying for a job that would help meet her needs, for which she would make an attractive candidate. I might also expect her to be more powerfully dissuaded from wasting her efforts applying for positions she could never hope to receive or keep. It would not surprise me in the least to find that a small shift of perspective—an "aha" moment or two—awakened the woman to how much cigarettes were costing her (on all kinds of levels). If the Spirit prompted these moments, I would also expect her to experience feelings of strength and assurance whenever her thoughts drifted to quitting. I would not be surprised to find that the Spirit was sending out "wake up calls" to the deadbeat dad, as well, inviting him to act more like a loving father. Perhaps images of his child would flash more frequently in his imagination or even his dreams. Perhaps thoughts of his ex-wife would connect him to a deeper place within him that felt peace and compassion for her rather than his usual contempt, quietly inviting him to come clean.

If the suggestions the Spirit sends us were less subtle, they would negate freewill and we would become little more than robots carrying out the will of our programmer. While their subtlety often makes them difficult to discern, these sweet-spot moments are more capable than we typically realize of signaling the way forward when we need to make a turn and helping us through heaps of trouble, provided we're paying attention.

DILLINGHAM AND THE DARK WOOD

During my college years I worked summers in a salmon cannery in Dillingham, Alaska. It wasn't exactly what I wanted to do with my time off, but Whitman College—a small, private liberal arts college in Walla Walla, Washington—was expensive, and I didn't have the money to pay for college beyond my first year.

Salmon saved me. Each year as millions of sockeye and other salmon migrated to the icy waters of Bristol Bay, I migrated with them. I secured a job as a Quality Assurance inspector on the canning line at Peter Pan Seafoods. The hours were brutal when the salmon were running and life was challenging. Yet in just six or seven short weeks, which often felt like the longest weeks of my life, I could return to Whitman with a sizeable check in hand. Combined with money made from student work, it would cover me for the year. Life was good, or so I thought.

By the summer following my hostel experience in Chinon, France, I was fully reconciled to the idea of attending seminary following my senior year of college. I was even enthusiastic. However, another significant challenge awaited me: I had to make it through my senior year of college—which first meant paying for it. Attending Whitman required that I provide a check for $8,000 each year beyond the financial aid, student loans, and modest parental assistance I received. This particular summer, I was a little more anxious for a big season than usual. My savings account had run completely dry by the time I walked off the plane in the remote, rough-and-ready fishing town of Dillingham. I was looking forward to putting a fire hose up to my savings account, turning the spigot, and blasting it with streams of cool, green cash.

Such was not to happen. Apparently the salmon decided to go on vacation that year, or maybe someone told them we were waiting to greet them with nets, sharp knives, little tin cans, and hot ovens and they didn't appreciate the hospitality. In any case, the cannery was sending us home early. After four weeks of scrounging around for any odd job I could find, I had managed to accumulate just $1,200.

As the date of my departure to the Lower 48 neared, I became more anxious and desperate as I struggled to reconcile my sense of call to ministry with the looming certainty that I couldn't afford to return for my final year of college. An internal storm was gathering on the horizon. The waves were getting choppy. My way forward appeared blocked by what felt like a hurricane heading straight for me. The hurricane felt particularly intense because I had experienced such a profound sense of call to the ministry while in France—a call that I had finally accepted after trying to run from it for so many years. I had at last begun to trust the lightning and thunder that lit up the path ahead and the liquid joy that beckoned me forward. Now it felt like the rug was being pulled out from under me. I wondered if I could ever trust my feelings and intuitions again, or if I might be massively deluded. All I knew for sure was that I was lost. Lost and scared.

On walks along Dillingham's bluffs overlooking the gray waters of Bristol Bay, I would cry out to God, "I need a miracle! I need another seven grand, and school starts in just seven weeks! Is there a lottery ticket I can buy? Is there some long-lost, wealthy relative out there who'd take pity on me? Is there a horde of salmon arriving that no one has spotted?" My cries simply disappeared into the void, returning unanswered. No assurance. No visions. And, of course, no money. The Dark Wood grew darker still.

Three days before my departure, I was standing out on the bluffs literally taking a breath from yelling at God for abandoning me in my final year of college, when a thought fluttered in and out of my mind almost before I could notice it. But I did notice. It said in essence, "You're asking me for the wrong thing. Don't ask for the money. Don't ask for a cheap trick to avoid defeat."

"Then what *should* I ask for?" I bellowed.

"Ask instead for assurance that I, whom you love so well, love you back, and that I will be there for you just as much in defeat as in victory."

My heart sank. I didn't want to even envision defeat. What would happen if that vision went out into the universe and was interpreted as advance acceptance of my doom? Or what if giving up on my dream would be interpreted as lack of confidence in God's goodness? I tried it anyway. What else could I do?

On my first half-hearted attempt, something unexpected drifted past my awareness: a whiff of peace. Nothing more than a faint whisper, but the first honest peace I'd felt in weeks. I became more sincere. Throughout the day I kept asking in various ways for the assurance that life would still be meaningful, and that God would still be there for me even if I could not afford to complete my college education. It took some time before I could truly feel it, and even longer to trust the feeling. When I finally did find it within me to tell God honestly that I desired God's presence in my life more than I wanted to finish college, an ocean of peace came rushing in that I have never forgotten. It washed over every anxiety, every fear, and every hurt I had so carefully held onto. It left me feeling like an immeasurable burden had been lifted from my shoulders. I walked back to the cannery a completely different person.

No longer absorbed in worry, I felt a sense of spaciousness and ease that allowed me to look around, listen, and absorb my surroundings. At one point I overheard someone talking about an upcoming opening of a salmon season in Southeastern Alaska. This one typically started later than the Bristol Bay season. I hadn't been aware of it before since I was normally working feverishly in the Dillingham cannery at that time.

Doing quick research, I learned that a cannery in Petersburg, Alaska, was hiring. They wouldn't promise me a job, but I figured that if I spent half the money I'd earned in Dillingham on a plane ticket to Petersburg, I might just get lucky.

Lightning flash: "You have nothing to lose!"

So I flew to Petersburg, turned in my application, and was hired the same day for a job on the cannery's Quality Assurance team. As fate, synchronicity, or just plain luck would have it, the salmon run in Southeastern Alaska turned out to be the largest in a century. For a solid month I worked from 6:30 a.m. until 1:30 or even 2:30 a.m. *every day.* The salmon nearly annihilated us! But at the end of the summer, I returned to Whitman College with $9,600 in my bank account. I think I had dark rings under my eyes as I made out my $8,000 check that fall but I'd never been so happy to pay.

I consider what happened that summer a miracle. Only the miracle wasn't finding the money, as some might conclude. While money made an enormous difference in finding my way back to school one year, the quiet assurance I received on those Dillingham Bluffs has become a defining moment in my life. For the last thirty years it has served as a waypoint in the Dark Wood reminding me when I've lost both my way and my grounding that the trees around me are not lost. My best way forward will most likely be found if I will just stand still and let *The Unexpected Love* find me.

You and I are not alone here. The world we inhabit is not just earth and sky, plants and animals. Funny things happen that add up to more. Every great religion has been formed, and continued, by those who have discovered it and wanted to know more. Most of us focus instead on life's practicalities—getting good grades, finding a good job, earning money to meet the next rent or mortgage payment, and using what's left over to provide safety and comfort for ourselves and those we care about. But this is not all your life is about. There is a realm of Spirit—what Jesus called the kingdom of God—that intersects our world, or as some say, *infuses* it. If this is true, it is the most exciting—and most meaningful thing of all. If there is no contact with the Holy Spirit, all religion is a sham. But if there is contact, it is the most important thing you will ever do.

SAMUEL THE PROPHET

The ancient Israelites were highly aware of this contact and of the strange synchronicity that tends to take shape when a yearning soul sends a signal to God that it's searching for home. They were also aware of how hard it is to interpret the lightning and thunder that connects our life's dots and points us in the right direction.

In the scene from *Bruce Almighty* recounted earlier, Bruce stays lost not because he has failed to ask from his heart to be found by God, but because he failed to *listen* that way. He expects an answer like in the movies, where the clouds part, a beam of sunshine falls on the protagonist's face, and he or she hears a voice booming from above. If an Israelite prophet were to offer advice to Bruce, I can imagine him saying, "Let God be God, not a movie version of God. And if you misinterpret the signals God sends, trust me: they'll keep coming, if only you'll watch and listen with as much soulfulness as you've invested in crying out to God." This is certainly the advice I imagine the prophet Samuel offering based on his life experience. Perhaps you will find a bit of your own story in Samuel's.

As the story goes in 1 Samuel 3, Samuel is alone one night, sleeping on the floor of the sanctuary, as was his duty as an assistant to the priest, Eli. Suddenly, Samuel hears a "voice" call to him, "Samuel, Samuel." Thinking the voice to be Eli's, Samuel calls out, "Here I am." Seeing no one around, he hurries to Eli's chamber. "Here I am, for you called me." Eli tells him he did not call, so Samuel returns to the Temple and falls asleep again. "Samuel, Samuel," he hears again. And again he goes to Eli. "Here I am, for you called me." Eli responds, "No, I did not. Go back and lie down again." At this point, the narrator jumps in to comment, "Now Samuel did not yet know the LORD, and the word of the LORD had not yet been revealed to him" (v. 7 NRSV). A third time, Samuel falls asleep only to hear his name called. Once more, he returns to Eli exclaiming, "Here I am, for you called me."

Now Eli suspects what's happening. He instructs Samuel, "Go, lie down; and if he calls you, you shall say, 'Speak, LORD, for your servant is listening.'" Once again, the voice calls out to Samuel. This time, he responds, "Speak, for your servant is listening" (vv. 9-10 NRSV). In response, Samuel receives a message that will eventually turn him from sanctuary assistant to the greatest prophet since

Moses. Shortly, Samuel's work would become critical for moving Israel from a ragtag band of loosely organized tribes being snuffed out of existence by surrounding enemies into a powerful nation. The first two kings of Israel—Saul and David—would be crowned as a result of Samuel's discernment. In other words, on this restless night as a clumsy sanctuary assistant, Samuel found his place in the world.

I find some important clues in this story of Samuel's call about the nature and character of God and how the Spirit helps us locate our next best steps. First, God acts in ways that are much more subtle than pagers and signs flashing in our face. While the narrator speaks of God calling Samuel as if there is an audible voice calling, this is Scripture's way of speaking of intuition. As noted earlier, rarely would an ancient Hebrew equate the "voice" of God with an audible sound. They knew that the signals are more subtle. It's like when a woman reveals her interest in a man by glancing at him in a certain way, laughing enthusiastically at his stupid jokes, perhaps brushing her hair to the side as she listens. When the guy's friend recounts the story later to their buddies he claims, "She was *screaming* at him to ask her out, but he was clueless!" Of course, she wasn't screaming. But she was.

When the Spirit pokes and prods us in its inaudible ways, particularly through gut hunches, intuitions, and shifts of awareness, a Hebrew narrator frequently recounts, "And God said such-and-such." That narrator is a lot like the guy recounting the story of his friend's cluelessness to their buddies. The clueless friend is a lot like Samuel. If the "voice" were as clear as an audible voice, wouldn't Samuel understand immediately that it was from God? In fact, even after Eli perceives what's going on and instructs Samuel to answer, "Speak, LORD, for your servant is listening," Samuel repeats every word but one. He says, "Speak, for your servant is listening," but leaves out the word *Lord*. This is classic Hebrew narrative technique indicating that Samuel still has his doubts. Yet despite his doubts about where the intuition is coming from, Samuel's heart is indeed open, and he is rewarded for continuing to listen. So are we. I wonder how many of us miss the Spirit calling us into great and wonderful work (or offering powerful help in a time of crisis) simply because we expect the signs to be more clear and for God to act with more supernatural bravado?

The second aspect of this story I find helpful is that the "voice" came to Samuel while he was alone, in the quietness of night. Sometimes the lightning flashes in our dreams. Other times, it flashes when we're alone and quiet, having put competing voices to rest. As William Blake once observed, "There is a moment in each Day which Satan cannot find."[3] I interpret this to mean that there's at least a moment in which the lightning and thunder are more likely to be perceived. It is most easily found when we've taken more than a few seconds to get quiet.

For nearly thirty years, I have made a practice of getting quiet for at least thirty minutes before I start my day. I clear any clutter that has accumulated in my "monkey mind" as the Buddhists call it, by stilling my mind and body. More important, I open my will to the Spirit as wide as I can get it. This creates a context in which the Spirit can act more freely since freewill is something the Spirit will not override. While I regularly experience the lightning and thunder during this morning ritual, often I receive no signals at all. I have kept this discipline for three decades, however, because it opens me more fully to the Spirit's promptings over the course of the day, particularly if I take a few seconds here and there to remind the Spirit (and myself) that I'm open to direction.

A third aspect I find instructive in Samuel's story is that Samuel receives *several* intuitive "hits," not just one. It's not like God gives up on him for mistaking the signals, even though Samuel keeps misinterpreting them. When it comes to finding our place in this world, mistakes don't matter nearly as much to God as they do to us, provided they're our own mistakes. We tend to make the most serious mistakes when we're trying to be someone else.

In my personal practice, this point is very important for a couple of reasons. It reminds me that the Spirit won't stop sending signals just because I happen to be unaware or have doubts. It also reminds me that, even after I believe I have picked up on a signal, I should take a step forward cautiously, as I might be mistaking one of my own voices for that of the Spirit. With each step forward, I remind the Spirit (and myself) that I'm still open to further direction and that I'm willing to take a step backward if asked.

The metaphor of the Dark Wood is instructive in this regard. When we listen for God's voice, it is as if we're walking in a forest at night. We may be "on our path" at the moment, but since the path is rarely straight or well-lit, it is not helpful to simply charge ahead assuming where it will lead. We may walk straight into a tree! Or over a cliff. Instead, we wait for the lightning, and for the call of the thunder to reveal the way forward. And it will. But usually only a small section of the path is revealed at a time. We walk to where we saw the path revealed and stop and wait for the lightning to signal the next step forward. It works much like the process of writing. As E. L. Doctorow once observed, "Writing a novel is like driving a car at night. You can only see as far as your headlights, but you can make the whole trip that way."[4]

Finally, a note of grace may be found in Samuel's story that's helpful, particularly when a few too many mistakes have been made by us or others and tension is high. The one who was instrumental in Samuel's finding his place in the world was Eli, who gently instructed him in how to listen and respond to God. Yet when Samuel receives his marching orders, as fate would have it, Samuel is called to inform Eli that Eli's ministry has come to an end. He has not served faithfully, so the word to Eli is a word of judgment upon him. When Samuel "hears" these words, he does not feel he has the strength to reveal them to Eli. (Who among us ever feels strong and confident enough to follow where the Spirit leads without a bit of extra encouragement or assurance?) Yet what gives Samuel the strength to proclaim the message is Eli's own urging. Eli instructs Samuel to speak what he has heard even after Samuel tells him why he's so reluctant.

What encourages me despite the story's sad ending for Eli is that, even though Eli has apparently been so unfaithful to his own sense of call that his ministry must come to an end, the story suggests that God's faithfulness is more potent than human unfaithfulness. We can be mediators of the Spirit's voice to others even when we haven't done such a great job at following it ourselves. Likewise, it reminds me that we can experience the Spirit's call even through the most imperfect people. Sometimes these people are our parents, or an out-of-touch minister, rabbi, or priest. They may even be our adversaries. Sometimes the imperfections we perceive in such mediators speak so loudly that we fail to hear or take seriously the deeper message they convey. How many messages and blessings have you received through an imperfect messenger? In the Dark Wood, even those who are lost themselves can be gift-bearers to others seeking their way in the dark.

6

THE GIFT OF TEMPTATION

We usually know what we can do,
but temptation shows us who we are.
—Thomas à Kempis

BY NOW YOU HAVE SPENT ENOUGH time exploring the Dark Wood to be aware that the obstacles life places before you may become opportunities for moving further along your path if you do not cower in fear and are receptive to the quiet promptings of the Spirit. Nowhere is this insight more important than when considering this next gift. Engaging meaningfully with it will do more to reveal your best path through the Dark Wood of life than any other. Yet it is also capable of undoing you if you aren't open and aware. The challenge posed by this gift is so formidable that even Jesus struggled with it.

This Dark Wood gift is that of temptation. By temptation, I do not have in mind anything on the standard list of high-minded moralists. No "sex, drugs, and rock n' roll," no greed, gluttony, or envy. No, what I mean is the temptation to do good. Yes, *good*, not evil.

Before you dismiss this claim out of hand, consider the last time you were seriously tempted to do something overtly sinister or evil. I'm not talking about the little things, like taking more than your fair share of dessert or gossiping a little more than you should about a coworker. And of course no one is immune to fantasies of doing great evil, such as throwing your boss out the window after being turned down for a promotion. Yet if you haven't actually thrown your boss out the window lately, or done more than entertain brief fantasies of such things, then doing great evil is probably not a significant temptation. If this statement is true for you, and if you are feeling far from your path, chances are that you've succumbed to the temptation of doing good somewhere along the way. In itself, doing good is not the problem. Doing the *wrong* good, however, is entirely the problem. By the *wrong good* I mean any good work that is not yours to do. It may be *someone else's* good to do, but not your own.

When David Whyte felt lost in his work at the nonprofit, for instance, he discovered that the good he was doing was not something he could do wholeheartedly. The work of a poet was more central to David's call in life, not the work of an administrator. Acting on the temptation to do the wrong good was what produced the exhaustion necessary to provoke David to ask questions about his work and seek counsel from a trusted friend. Eventually, exhaustion drove David to take the enormous risk of trading a steady job (and paycheck) for a chance to swim in his elemental waters as a poet. He has been wholeheartedly swimming there ever since.

Let's pause for a moment and consider some implications. David Whyte is a man of high intelligence, whose strategic mind is as keen as any other I know. Yet for all his intelligence and ability, what led David to find his distinctive calling, giving him the courage to take the plunge into his elemental waters, had little to do with intelligence or strategic ability. In terms of finding his place in this world, exhaustion proved to be a greater gift than all the others.

The reason the Dark Wood gift of temptation is so important is that it produces results—like exhaustion—that reveal fairly quickly whether you are on a path that is central to who you are and what you're here for or are on a side path. The faculties people typically employ to discern these very things—logic, reason, and strategy—tend to be surprisingly unhelpful in this regard. In fact, they often produce a long list of reasons we should stay on a path that is not our own and not make waves. Logic and reason will say, "Think of all the *good* you're doing working here!" You may not be working for a nonprofit trying to save the world, but your strategic mind may advise, "Think of all the people who rely on you. Think of your coworkers. If not them, then think of your family. Ensuring that they have food to eat and a roof over their heads is a good thing. And what about your pension? Why not put off doing what you really feel drawn to do for a few more years? When you retire you can do anything you want!" Of course, by the time many people retire they are so used to doing what everyone else wants of them that they have lost all concept of who they are and what they want—or how to say no. So instead they pick up a television remote in one hand and a golf club in the other and call it "the *good* life." It seems like the most "reasonable" thing to do.

Finding your distinctive path in life involves more than applying reason, logic, and strategy. It requires instinct and imagination. Instinct because the surest sign that you're on your path is not reason alone but wholeheartedness. Imagination because your true place in this world tends to be found just beyond the edges of your immediate awareness. It's a bit like walking in the dark. In a very real sense, you do not find your path. Your path *finds you*. More precisely, the path that fits you best is *revealed* to you.

You may object that if your path is so well suited to you, you should be able to figure out what it is on your own. Shouldn't you be able to make an inventory of your aptitudes and interests and find an occupation or lifestyle that best makes use of them? If finding your path worked like this, then any number of career inventories could ferret out a few of your interests and aptitudes, suggest occupations best suited to them, and set you on your way. Your chances of finding "good" work through such means are reasonable, particularly if using a sophisticated (often costly) evaluative tool administered by a trained psychologist or career counselor. Yet your chances of finding your life's meaning and purpose and connecting these things to the good work you are specifically called to do are about as poor as winning the lottery.

Partly, this is because your calling is more than just your occupation. Your occupation may very well become—and hopefully *will* become—a central channel through which you live into your calling, if it hasn't already. After all, it's what you do for half of your waking life, so of course it could be a central channel. But your occupation is not the same as your path or calling.

For example, my occupation is "minister." My ministry is definitely a central channel through which I live into my calling. It brings me alive better than any vocation I can possibly imagine. And I have imagined a great many alternatives, I assure you! If I were to take a vocational inventory (I have), it would likely indicate that ministry is one of several potential careers that would be a good fit for me (it did). But, so what?

There are a thousand different ways of being a minister. A minister might be more of a "mothering parent" than a "fiery prophet," for instance, or might be better suited to a small country church than a large church in the city. Within the Protestant faith alone, there are at least six hundred different denominations in which to practice ministry, some of which have extremely different understandings of what it means to be a Christian. And if there are a thousand ways of being a minister, there are many more areas of potential focus. A minister may serve a church, teach at a college, or run a homeless shelter, for instance. Even within a church, a minister might focus more on teaching than preaching, or on administration over youth work. And then consider how many different messages might constitute the handful that are central to a person's ministry. It has been said that preachers have just three or four sermons they preach throughout their careers—they simply find different ways of preaching them each week. So those messages had better be well chosen!

All these nuances to a single occupation should suggest loud and clear that finding your place in the world is more than just finding something "good" to do with your time and energy. Finding and following your path is an ongoing process that tends to take shape, bit by bit, over many years, often by trial and error. It evolves, requiring an ongoing conversation between your body, soul, community of friends, loved ones, those you serve, and the Spirit to discern where it lies at any particular moment. Along the way, the temptation to do the wrong good is one of the greatest gifts you can receive, as it continually challenges you to discern between the good you are *called* to do and the good you are specifically *not called* to do. More often than not, your intuition—your deep listening to the voice of the Spirit—is a better judge than your logic, reason, or strategic ability. Thus, the gift of temptation also refines your listening ability like no other—often through suffering the consequences of acting against your intuition. Trial by fire.

DOING THE WRONG GOOD, PART 1: MY BAD

In the summer of 2005, I learned more than I ever cared to know about the shortcomings of privileging logic, reason, and strategy over intuitive listening. I learned by doing precisely the good that I was not called to do and living with the result. That year I was busily preparing for a cross-country walk that would take place in the spring and summer of 2006. A number of us were tired of the hatred, intolerance, and anger spread by self-proclaimed spokespeople for Christianity in the media. We wanted to offer a vision for a more inclusive, open, and joyous faith taking shape at the grassroots of our nation. Anchoring our walk was a magnificent document drafted by dozens of clergy, laypeople, biblical scholars, and theologians from around the country who sought to articulate a way of being Christian that moved well beyond the extremes of both conservatism and liberalism. The document eventually became known around the world as "The Phoenix Affirmations." These affirmations consisted of twelve principles that take seriously the three great loves (God, neighbor, self) that Jesus identified when he observed that the two greatest commandments are to love God with heart, mind, soul, and strength and to love your neighbor as yourself. (A complete list of the twelve Phoenix Affirmations can be found in the appendix.)

The important thing to understand for our purposes is not the affirmations themselves but the fact that The Phoenix Affirmations were not widely known at the time. This largely unknown, single-page document was to serve as the theological underpinning of the whole effort, which was being undertaken by scores of individuals and 150 different faith communities. We all felt that some form of commentary should be produced to show that The Phoenix Affirmations came from the heart of Christian faith, not just the fringe. This job fell to me.

There wasn't much time. I had just four weeks' vacation in August of 2005 to devote to writing the entire book. Given the lengthy process required to put a book into national circulation, submitting the manuscript in September pushed the anticipated publication date dangerously close to the commencement of the walk the following April. So when my family traveled to our small cabin on the Oregon Coast that August, I was on a mission. You might say, following the Blues Brothers, that I was on a "mission from God." Or at least, I *thought* I was. Over the next four weeks, I wrote in sheer panic, starting hours before my wife and daughters arose in the morning and stopping long after they'd gone to bed.

The full weight of my responsibility was ever upon me. Most of our core group of walkers had quit their jobs or taken unpaid leaves of absence just to devote themselves to making this walk a reality. Other people had made sacrificial financial donations, or devoted long hours of work after their day jobs were finished, or both, out of belief in the project.

"I've got to come through for these people and this cause," I thought to myself each time I was tempted to take a little time away from my computer.

All month long, I ignored my family and the many friends and relatives who passed through for a visit. Needless to say, I was not exactly Mr. Popularity at the cabin that summer, not even among those who believed strongly in the cause. Quietly, I resented the fact that no one could seem to understand the pressure I was under to write a whole book in a scant four weeks.

As much as this pressure and resentment set me on edge, however, a different, unexpected issue was gnawing at me even more: Those flashes of lightning and claps of thunder I've been writing about were coming at me regularly, but they were all prodding me to relax, play with my family, and not worry *one bit* about the book! In other words, they indicated the exact opposite of what I "knew" to be true.

You can imagine the level of skepticism these intuitions engendered. "How can this be?" I kept asking myself. "Am I going crazy or am I just lazy?" Setting the book aside and playing with my family would have been the "easy" thing to do. Yet the intuitions kept coming. More than I resented others for wanting me to relax, I resented myself for being so "weak" as to even entertain the idea that intuitions could be genuine.

Going on the walk was clearly part of what it meant for me to live into my sweet spot. So was authoring a book on the Affirmations before the walk began. This is still as clear to me now as it was back then. Thus, it seemed equally clear that the right, good, and logical thing to do on vacation that summer was to devote myself to writing the book. So I shoved the intuitions aside, deciding to stay the course and buckle down with even greater resolve to get the book written.

In the midst of wrestling with these conflicting feelings, I found myself out on the beach one day to clear my head. There, I came across an unusual sight: a twenty-foot wooden piling three feet thick was lying on its side high on a sand dune, having been tossed there by the raging storms of the previous winter. I stood in awe as I considered the force of the waves that could snap such a strong piling like a toothpick and leave it high on the beach.

Just a few feet from the piling I discovered something even more amazing: a lightbulb. From the whitish haze covering the clear glass bulb, it was obvious that the lightbulb had weathered the same winter storms as the piling. Only this lightbulb, delicate as it was, had survived the storms completely intact!

Suddenly the thought hit me: "If you are to survive this ordeal, you must be more like the lightbulb than the piling. Let go of your rigidity, which will only serve you like it did this piling, and flow with the storm like this lightbulb."

Wave after wave of peace and joy welled up within me, so strong that I sank to my knees in the sand and wept. Only, I am embarrassed to say that by the time I arrived back at the cabin where my laptop awaited me, my fear got the best of me. I decided that the insight must not apply to my present situation but to the coming year back home. I rigidly held my ground on the writing project, determined to finish the book by the end of vacation.

By the time we headed home at the end of August, I had spent not a single day with my family. But I'd written a whopping 240 pages on the Phoenix Affirmations! There was one problem, however, besides the fact that I was exhausted and everyone was mad at me: I had written 240 pages on only the first four Affirmations. While I had intended to write on all twelve, it seemed that more depth was needed, so I figured I'd propose to the publisher that this book be the first of a trilogy.

After submitting the book, I received the publisher's verdict quickly. Essentially, they said, "We love the Phoenix Affirmations, but you've written the wrong book." They argued that people would never commit to reading three books on the Phoenix Affirmations without knowing what they were or being convinced that they were important. In other words, my August book-writing odyssey had been a nearly complete waste of effort. The publisher said they'd be willing to publish a book on the Affirmations, but only if it was on all twelve and *no more than 150 pages*. And I would have to submit the entire draft in the next six weeks if the book had any hope of being published in time for the walk! My heart sank. I felt like that piling on the beach: snapped like a toothpick.

Now, in full realization of my painful mistake, and in the awareness that the storm was now raging around me more than ever, I decided to let go and be more like the lightbulb than the piling. I would flow wherever the Spirit would take me.

Whereas in Oregon the flow had clearly been toward taking time off with my family, now in Arizona that flow took me in an entirely different direction. Like a tide moving out to sea where it had just moments before been heading in toward land, the path of my deepest peace and quiet joy led me back out into the fray of book writing. I asked the church council for permission to take my two remaining weeks of study-leave for the year immediately, and to allow me some extra writing time once I returned to work, in an effort to meet the publishing deadline. Even though I had returned home from Oregon exhausted from my work, now it was energizing and delighting me. The flow had changed. I was drawing seemingly inexhaustible energy from it, letting go of my fear and drifting where the Spirit was beckoning me.

Over the next several weeks, my writing came faster and more easily than it ever has. I submitted a solid draft for a 150-page book on the Phoenix Affirmations by the publishing deadline. Happily, this book was far better than my first attempt. To this day it is my most widely read work.

It is said that hindsight is 20/20. Looking back, it is clear that if I had followed the intuitions that had been with me the entire month of August, I still would have written a book on the Phoenix Affirmations, released it in time for the walk, *and* I could have relaxed and played with my family. It makes perfect sense in hindsight why I would have been called to spend significant time with my family, for in the coming year I would spend almost no time at all with them. The burdens of creating a nonprofit organization, fund-raising, route-planning, forming partnerships with other organizations, creating public awareness, and physical preparation all while continuing to serve as a minister at my church, placed strains on me and the family that would test our family bonds for all they were worth. Undoubtedly, spending meaningful time with my family that August would have made the year ahead easier for all of us. Yet taking this time would not have been something I could have figured out on my own using reason, logic, or strategic thinking. All of us—including my family—*knew* that the only time the book could be written was on vacation that summer. The Spirit knew otherwise.

I accomplish more and am happier doing it when I pay less attention to doing the "right" thing and pay more attention to those sweet-spot moments that reveal what I am called to do. Since the summer of 2005, I have been firmly resolved to take these signals more seriously than ever before, particularly when they all point in the same direction. My general rule of thumb is, the higher the risk, the more confirmation is needed before moving forward. And if confirmation comes, move ahead boldly until or unless proven otherwise.

DOING THE WRONG GOOD, PART 2: JESUS, BLAKE, AND THE ADVERSARY

I would feel far worse about wrestling with the temptation to do the wrong good if not for the fact that my struggle is shared by someone I respect and admire greatly: Jesus. If you wrestle with this temptation yourself, perhaps you will find comfort in knowing that this was Jesus' greatest temptation in life, too. What? You've never heard of Jesus being tempted to do the wrong good before? You'll find it in the story of Jesus' temptations in the wilderness. His story offers insight for overcoming this significant obstacle.

After his baptism in the Jordan River, it is said that Jesus entered the dry and barren wilderness where for forty days he fasted and was tempted by Satan, or the "Adversary" in Hebrew. As the story goes, the Adversary first challenged Jesus to turn stone into bread. Jesus refused, stating that humans do not live by bread alone. Next, the Adversary showed Jesus all the cities and kingdoms of the world, claiming they'd be his if Jesus just bowed down and worshiped him. Jesus refused, declaring that we are to worship God alone. Finally, the Adversary took Jesus to the highest point of the Jerusalem Temple, challenging him to jump off and let angels save him. Again, Jesus refused, stating, "Don't test the Lord your God." Defeated, the Adversary left Jesus to await "the next opportunity" (Luke 4:12-13).

The most insightful depiction of Jesus' temptations that I have ever seen is *The Second Temptation* by the English poet, painter, and printmaker William Blake. Blake's painting depicts a pious-looking man standing to the left of Jesus, who for all appearances could be a Hebrew prophet like Moses or Elijah. The man points up toward the heavens with one hand and down to the world's cities with the other. Jesus stands calmly to the right pointing in the same two directions. If you did not know the painting was of Jesus' temptations you might not realize that the man on the left is the Adversary. No horns, fangs, or pitchforks give him away, nor does his demeanor look the slightest bit sinister. If anything, the man looks pious and sincere.

Here Blake displays his insight. Blake recognizes that someone with the spiritual stature of Jesus would be even less tempted by overt evil than we are. If you were the Adversary and wanted to tempt someone like Jesus, you'd have to convince Jesus you were on his side while rolling out the biggest temptations you could possibly muster. All your temptations would have to be about *doing good*. Let's consider the specific goods Jesus was tempted by:

- turning stone into bread
- ruling the world
- performing impressive miracles

These temptations seem pretty harmless, don't they? If Jesus would base his ministry on turning stone into bread, he could not only feed himself (not a great temptation for the Messiah of God) but also *feed all the hungry of the world*. (Now we're talking!) If Jesus held all political power, the ego trip would not have been a significant temptation for Jesus, but imagine the temptation of being able to change a few of the world's laws, or directing public and private resources to their best use, or creating world peace? Then again, if Jesus could impress people with some extravagant public miracles, like jumping off the Temple roof and surviving, he may not find the boost in public esteem very tempting but surely the prospect of converting everyone and making them disciples would be. No longer would belief be necessary. Miracles would provide certainty.

The point is none of these activities would harm anyone. Not initially, anyway. And Jesus does feed the hungry, change the political equation, and perform miracles at various points in his ministry. Yet none of these individual activities were ones that Jesus was called to devote all his time and energy to. Like the Ring of Power in Tolkien's *Lord of the Rings*, if wielded by someone like Jesus, these gifts might do enormous good for the world but would ultimately enslave both their wielder and those he was trying to help.

The problem is, as we've seen, there is a world of difference between doing good, and doing the specific good that you are called to do. The Spirit beckons us not to be good, but to be human—humble, of the *humus*—which ultimately means finding your elemental waters, which are connected to God, and living into your fullest energies. You can (and will) do a lot of good by walking the path that brings you most fully alive in this world, but in order to stay on this path, you must learn to say no to doing a great many "good" things.

Jesus' purpose and true power was not realized through

feeding the hungry or practicing politics or performing miracles, even as each of these surely was a *part* of his path. Devoting his entire life's work to them was too small a calling for Jesus. God called him to something far higher. Part of Jesus' calling was to live more fully into his *human identity* than anyone else had ever done before. In so doing, Jesus reveals how much the rest of us resemble Pinocchio by comparison—how much we're not our true selves. Jesus also reveals that the more we draw from the Source of our highest energies, thereby living into our true identity, the more we resemble actual divinity. That's because in order to follow our best path in the world, we've got to move off the path of common wisdom and start following a path marked by God's lightning flashes and thunder claps—those gut hunches and reverberations of peace and joy that emanate from the Spirit.

My friend Bruce often observes that the question is not "Are you *saved*?" The question is, "Are you *used*?" In other words, have you given yourself over to the Spirit in such a way that you are willing to allow it to lead you on your path and bring you to fullness of life? Are you willing to move beyond the protestations of your logical, strategic mind, and your desire to figure out everything for yourself, to follow the sweet-spot moments that reveal where your soul yearns to travel in this world in conversation with God? Many people never allow themselves the joy of following their best path because they think it would be too enjoyable and therefore selfish. They assume it is more godly and self-sacrificing to follow a path that is not central to their deepest yearnings, never considering that God has placed these yearnings within them for a reason.

While they may not know the reason, God does. When the Christian Scriptures speak of becoming a "new creation," what they mean is surrendering to God's intention for our lives by following the path of our greatest aliveness. When they speak of entering the kingdom of God, they refer to the place where your elemental waters reside and you engage with life wholeheartedly.

THE MYTH OF THE ADVERSARY OR WHAT THE HECK DO WE DO NOW?!

In the mythological imagination of Jewish and Christian lore—lore not contained in the Bible, incidentally—the Adversary who tempted Jesus to do the wrong good started his career as God's highest angel. He had drunk the Kool-Aid. He was with God's program. He wanted to make the earth a wonderful place to be. I find this insight into the origin of the Adversary helpful. For whether or not one believes in the literal existence of the Adversary, or Satan, the mythological archetype of the Adversary's origin helps better define both the struggle, and the gift, of our temptation to do the wrong good.

The story of what created the problem between God and the Adversary is unclear, as there are a number of differing versions in the lore. So, I'll offer you *my own* version, which is closely based on a combination of the others, in order to better understand the mythology and the way it describes not something that happened long ago, but something that keeps happening up to our present day.

The rift occurred when the Adversary became convinced

that God was overly optimistic about God's creation, particularly human beings. The Adversary knew that human beings were supposed to live in harmony with God, but that they contained two flaws that kept them from doing so, thus making them less than human. Those flaws were pride and shame, both of which convince us that we are separate from God, either because we are smarter than God or because we are so unworthy of God's love, and therefore must create our own path through life. As long as humanity followed only the path it knew well and understood, it would never achieve the stature or majesty that was meant for it. Thus, no matter how good they started out, human beings would soon devolve into ugly shells of themselves. They would become cruel and hateful. There would be strife and mayhem, even warfare. And the Adversary wanted peace and harmony as much as God wanted it, at least at first.

The Adversary was aware that human beings could overcome this flaw by letting go of pride and shame, and allowing God to set them on the path of their true identity. Yet he also knew that most people would have neither the will nor the courage to follow this path, even though God would surely make them aware of its existence. This is because their true path led off the bright, well-trod road and into a deep Dark Wood where they could not see the way clearly. While their hearts would continually yearn for this path, it would appear impossible to follow so long as they were convinced that it was up to them to find their way in the dark or that they were unworthy of following that path once it was found.

Knowing how badly humanity would mess things up if they

tried to wander through the Dark Wood on their own, the Adversary came alongside humanity to guide them. Only, because the Adversary was no longer living in harmony with God, he could not see into the darkness any better than the humans could. Unable to guide humans along their true path, the Adversary did the "next best thing." He created broad, bright roadways and paved, well-ordered sidewalks that were easy to follow. As long as they stuck to these roads and sidewalks, they would never become fully human, but neither would human society devolve into chaos and mayhem. In fact, following the bright and easy way, humans could do a lot of good for themselves and each other.

Yet, when humans started following these well-ordered roads and sidewalks, their hearts could still sense that there were paths in the darkness that led to their true place in the world. They could hear music emanating from those woods sounding not unlike the liquid joy of thirty French ballerinas talking. Fear was the only thing keeping them from daring to step out of their familiar world and explore the woods. And because humans were ultimately creations of God, not the Adversary, they yearned for these paths mightily, becoming increasingly unhappy, anxious, and belligerent.

"Humans may yet fall into anarchy!" exclaimed the Adversary one day. Wanting above all else to keep things decent and in order, he set up taverns along the good and proper roads he'd constructed. There, humans could drink their fill on cheap beer that would mimic the *sensation* of liquid joy that comes from following one's true path, yet without being anywhere near it. The Adversary knew we would make all kinds of vows to follow our true path under the influence of the beer, but when morning came, and it was cold and wet outside, and our heads throbbed so badly from our excesses the night before, and the fireplace in the tavern was so warm and inviting, we'd say to ourselves, "I'll just have a drink or two until the weather clears." And so it would go.

Some of these taverns eventually took the form of churches and other houses of worship, where religious leaders served the high-octane beer of self-righteousness, which seemingly offered the highest of highs. Serving their special brew, they convinced their flocks that the Dark Wood was evil, and that if they did not renounce their yearning to explore the Dark Wood and grant their assent to a strict code of doctrine and dogma, they would be burned with fire for eternity. Further, the preachers promised their drunk followers that if they just stayed in line, they would be rewarded with "fullness of life." There was no need to enter the darkness to search around for some path that "will only get you lost." While this "fullness of life" seemed pretty empty, the preachers promised their flocks that all they had to do was keep coming back to the tavern-churches and they would enter paradise after they died. In so doing, the Adversary turned himself into God and God into the enemy.

What the Adversary did not realize, however (probably because he drank his own booze), was that God had a backup plan for those who had lost themselves in this way. God had given humanity a gift that is more powerful than any booze. It was a dangerous gift, however. Not everyone would respond to it in the same way or in a helpful manner. So God planted this gift far enough down in people's souls that it could only be accessed when people were living so far from their path that their humanity had worn down far enough to uncover it. That gift was Despair. God knew that as long as the Adversary's preachers and other tavern owners continued to serve their booze, they might pacify their flocks for quite some time, but eventually they would begin to feel Despair. Once Despair set in, no amount of booze could make it disappear. The danger was that some humans would utterly break down under the power of Despair and do more harm to themselves than good, particularly if the Adversary caught on to what was happening. Yet to prevent the Adversary from simply having his way with people, God did another unexpected thing. Remembering Blake's quotation earlier: God created "a moment in each Day which [the Adversary] cannot find."[1] It was a moment of grace that provided the possibility for people to get a glimpse of what life could be like if they lived free of the Adversary's interference.

With cheap beer no longer placating them, and desperation setting in, many people would no longer be content to remain in the taverns. In those brief moments where the Adversary lost sight of them, these people might dare to venture outside into the howling wind and pouring rain. Finally outside the taverns, they'd soon find themselves on the edge of the Dark Wood where they could sense something mysterious calling to them. Being desperate enough to follow any path but the one they were on, some would stumble half drunk into the darkness. At these moments, lightning would crackle across the sky, illuminating a path before them. Thunder would clap its hands, sending reverberations of peace and joy through their bodies which they hadn't felt in years. The music of ten thousand souls singing freely and easily would fill their ears and they would take a step forward onto the path the lightning had just revealed. There, within the dark sanctuary of the Great Unknown they would discover themselves in the world's embrace, lightning and thunder flashing and clapping all around them, in the eye of a perfect storm.

Their path through the Dark Wood would rarely be clear or certain, but those souls who dared to follow it would know it to be *their* path. While these souls would never rid themselves of restlessness or yearning, life in the Dark Wood would evoke a sense of peace, joy, and lightness of being such as they had never experienced following the Adversary's wide, brightly lit roads and paved, well-marked streets. The Adversary's highways and byways might lead them to the next tavern, but the Dark Wood's paths would lead them home.

7

THE GIFT OF
DISAPPEARING

Strategic Withdrawal: any act you can devise, any psycho-
spiritual act at all, that embodies a willingness to wait for the
world to disclose itself to you, rather than to disclose yourself,
your altruism, your creativity, skills, energy, ideas and (let's face
it) agenda, myopia, preconceptions, delusions, addictions and
inappropriate trajectories to the world.

—David James Duncan

PRIDE ARTIFICIALLY INFLATES OUR self-image. Shame artificially deflates it. Both tend to set us on dead-end paths because
they cause us to willingly obstruct our connection with God. Pride
convinces us that we are better off living under our own power
and authority. Shame convinces us that God does not love us as we
are, thus we are unworthy of connection. Ironically, both pride and
shame tend to fabricate an image of ourselves that is ultimately too
small to live within. Too small because it is restricted by the limits
of our imagination, which itself is limited by the cultural norms of

our surroundings, historical context, family upbringing, personal fears and insecurities, and so on. Even when pride builds us up with visions of grandeur, those images tend to be inherently unstable. Built upon a foundation of insecurity and wishful-thinking, even small challenges tend to collapse them like a house of cards.

Humility is what keeps us grounded in reality. It is also the quality that best ensures that the internal images that shape our lives—images that influence us as parents, spouses, professionals, spiritual seekers, and so forth—will be large enough to allow us to move freely in the world rather than cage us in. In chapter 3 we found that true humility has nothing to do with self-debasement before others. Rather, humility is the quality that gave an outcast like Moses the courage to bow down before no other power but God and to demand that Pharaoh free the Hebrew slaves. Humility is living by God's vision of you, not your own. God sees a lot more of you than you do. Consequently, God sees a lot more to love, putting your shortcomings against a far larger backdrop than you can. God also sees the kind person you are capable of growing into when you live wholeheartedly. It is this wholehearted image of yourself that feels most like home when you glimpse it even for the briefest moment.

The Dark Wood gift of disappearing helps us maintain a healthy distance from self-conceptions that are either built upon a grand house of cards or upon a meager image pulled from the swamps of shame. More than most, this gift provides us a certain spaciousness and grace to move about life freely, following those sweet-spot moments that mark our path even when significant obstacles are placed before us. Few of us, however, claim this gift or use it skillfully.

TOBAR PHADRAIC

In a poem entitled "Tobar Phadraic" ("Patrick's Well"), named after an ancient sacred well in Ireland where Saint Patrick is said to have visited, David Whyte admonishes the reader to do something unusual:

> *Turn sideways into the light as they say*
> *the old ones did and disappear into the originality*
> *of it all. Be impatient with explanations*
> *and discipline the mind not to begin*
> *questions it cannot answer.*[1]

As Whyte explains it, the concept of turning sideways into the light is a reference to a mythological people called the *Tuatha Dé Danann* in Irish lore. As he explains it, they were a small, somewhat fragile, but immensely magical people who lived in Ireland before the arrival of human beings (probably the predecessors of leprechauns in Irish mythology). With the coming of humans, the *Tuatha Dé Danann* became agitated, as they found humanity's ways coarse and barbaric. Being a gentle people, they chose not to oppose humans. Rather, at one point, they are said to have simply "turned sideways into the light and disappeared."

Whyte draws on this mythic tradition to advise his readers to refuse to give in to any power that seeks to give us a name or identity that is too small for us. His admonition to be impatient with explanations and unanswerable questions is not anti-intellectual but is born out of the awareness of the seductive allure of false images. They can be mesmerizing, especially when we stick around long enough either to defend or explain ourselves. It's a little like answering the question, "When did you stop beating your mother?" You're doomed the moment you even try to answer the question. Just disappear, advises Whyte, before a powerful false self has enough time to cast its spell on you.

Free of its power, Whyte advises that we seek a place where the world *around* us can call forth something deep from the world *within* us in a way that points toward our highest identity. In Whyte's poem, such a place of power is represented by *Tobar Phadraic*, a place where pilgrims have come to commune with the holy for centuries.

> *Walk the green road*
> *above the bay and the low glinting fields*
> *toward the evening sun. Let that Atlantic*
> *gleam be ahead of you and the gray light*
> *of the bay below you,*
> *until you catch, down on your left,*
> *the break in the wall,*
> *for just above in the shadow*
> *you'll find it hidden, a curved arm*
> *of rock holding the water close to the mountain,*
> *a just-lit surface smoothing a scattering of coins,*

and in the niche above, notes to the dead
and supplications for those who still live.

Finally, when standing in a place of greatest potential to properly name us, Whyte speaks of a moment when we sense that the barrier between the human and divine is thin. Then we dare to let this place stir within us a revelation of our true identity and purpose. Do not ask for healing in this sacred place, Whyte warns, for this only empowers your false self's sense of shame and desire to be "fixed." Rather, stand empty and open to the world as you stood toward it as a child. Let it speak to you of your unique place in the world.

Now you are alone with the transfiguration
and ask no healing for your own
but look down as if looking through time,
as if through a rent veil from the other
side of the question you've refused to ask,

and remember how as a child
your arms could rise and your palms
turn out to bless the world.

While Whyte's poem envisions standing in a place of fierce beauty and ancient holiness to evoke a revelation of our identity, such revelations can come to us in places that appear quite ordinary. The key is to refuse to let any situation or circumstance mark you in a way that does not reflect your highest identity. You must disappear. Instead, stand "as a child" (reappear) with your palms turned out to accept an identity only in situations or circumstances that call forth the very best within you.

DISAPPEARING

I learned the art of disappearing and reappearing the hard way from a pastoral search committee I faced in Omaha, Nebraska, in 1995, while finishing my doctorate at Princeton Theological Seminary. In my denomination, ministers are not moved around by bishops or other church leaders. Instead, a committee from the church is formed to discern who their new minster should be and interviews the candidate extensively. The committee's choice is then brought before the congregation for a vote, usually after the candidate delivers a "candidating sermon."

As a young seminarian just starting out in the ministry, I was fortunate to gain the attention of several congregations around the country. A handful interviewed me and offered to take me before the congregation as their chosen candidate. But I'd spent enough time in the Dark Wood to know that you aren't likely to find a path to which you can devote yourself wholeheartedly unless the lightning flashes and the thunder claps repeatedly deep within, indicating that the path forward has something to do with living into your greater identity. While I had serious interest in each of these congregations, none of them called to me in this way so I simply gritted my teeth and waited. Far better to live with a little uncertainty over future employment than to pick up and move across the country to do the wrong good in the wrong place.

Not long afterward, a church in Omaha, Nebraska, contacted me. From the moment we started talking, I could feel an electrical storm brewing. One thing led to another, and by the time I was invited for a formal interview before the committee in Omaha, that storm was raging inside. While my wife, Melanie, and I had never been to the Midwest, and admittedly had never taken an interest in living there, the thunder kept calling over and over to both of us, "This is your place!"

Ahead of our visit, I was keenly aware that the committee, as interested as they were, would be skeptical of my ability to take the reins as their new senior minister. The only position I'd held, aside from my student work in seminary, was as a part-time minister of a church of twenty-five members in Closter, New Jersey, while I was finishing my doctoral dissertation. The Omaha congregation was nine hundred members.

The thought of missing my opportunity to serve a congregation I was so powerfully drawn to terrified me. How would I ever convince them that I had what it takes? In preparation, I thought through every possible question the committee might ask and how to answer it. I thought of ways to characterize my lack of experience as a strength and to show them that serving a large church would be easy for a bright, intelligent guy like me.

During the actual interview, I remember being unusually impressed with myself. I'd accurately predicted their questions and was therefore able to draw on the vast bank of material I'd constructed for my responses. At times, I noticed smiles and flickers in people's eyes that clearly suggested that they were thinking, "This is our minister!" I walked out of the interview having done what author and speaker Tony Campolo says he does when he preaches unusually well: "I was so good I was taking notes on *myself*!" I knew I was being called to this Omaha congregation and that I'd proven that I was, without doubt, the best person to serve it.

The committee felt otherwise.

Learning of their decision several days later, I was devastated. "But God *called* me to this church! How could they not see this as clearly as I did?" Wondering what fatal flaw I might have that would cause me to lose the position I was so certain was meant for me, and seeking to provide some sense of closure to my grief, I called the search committee chair asking if she might share why I wasn't offered the position. I had a number of interviews scheduled with other churches and I didn't want to make the same mistakes.

There was a pause at the other end of the line. I could tell the committee chair was honoring my request by thinking through her response carefully before speaking. I'd had enough conversations with her to know that she sincerely liked me and would give me an honest response. Finally, in a voice cracking with a hint of disappointment, she said, "Well, I think you could have been less sure of yourself." That was all she offered. And that was all she needed to say. Her words cut me to the quick. She was *exactly* right. In acting so cocksure of myself and my ability to lead a nine-hundred-member church without any significant prior experience, I actually painted a perfectly clear picture that I lacked the one thing that would be most essential to leading their congregation: *an awareness of how much I did not know.*

The search committee knew something I would not realize until much later: that even the most seasoned leaders know little about leading a congregation that does not stand in need of revising moment by moment. To assume that one has the task of leadership all figured out would signal not only the downfall of the minister, but of the church.

I thought to myself, "How ironic that if I'd actually let down my guard with the search committee and revealed not just how excited I was, but how nervous and unprepared I felt about leading a church of their size, they may have had more confidence in my ability to do just that!"

What really hurt was the realization that I actually did have the characteristic they were looking for. I was keenly aware of my ignorance. I knew full well that I'd have to adjust my plans in light of changing circumstances and that I would need to seek the counsel of many wise people and the Holy Spirit to help me discern each step of the way. But I showed none of this to the committee.

I blew it.

If you think this self-assessment is overly harsh, I can assure you that I did, in fact, make a significant error of judgment. Softening the assessment doesn't make it any less true. As best I can understand, even with the benefit of hindsight, the Spirit had called me to Omaha. The lightning and thunder could not have made this more clear. And just when it mattered most, I stood physically before the search committee, but internally I really wasn't standing before them at all. As in David Whyte's poem, I stood before an image of my false self, one that was bright and handsome, whose adoring smile concealed a faint smirk as he whispered to me, "You know, don't you, that you are only loved to the extent that you are perfect?" I wanted the committee to love me a lot, so I gladly allowed this image to place its mark on me.

Far better to have "turned sideways into the light and disappeared" before this image. Then I could have stood before them, humble as a child with palms turned out, as Whyte suggests, ready to join them in blessing the world. They may have named my calling.

For a good long while after that experience, I wondered what God thought of me, or if God even still cared. I wondered, too, against my better nature, if God might punish me. Punishment seemed like a good and right decision since I wanted so badly to punish *myself*. Do you ever entertain feelings like this, or am I the only one?

While I harbored no fears of ultimate retribution after my failure in Omaha, it did seem logical that God, though still loving me, might relegate me to the B-side of life or ship me off to the church equivalent of the Island of Misfit Toys to play out my career. I couldn't help wondering, how exactly *does* God respond when you fail in ways that matter both to you and the world?

THE UNEXPECTED RESPONSE

When it comes to mistakes that keep me from walking my best path, I tend to learn quickly. And despite my fear that God might never call to me again, another powerful electrical storm developed that brought me to a congregation in Scottsdale, Arizona. From the start, it seemed that the Scottsdale Congregational Church search committee thought I could do no wrong. White it might have been tempting not to say or do anything that would disabuse them of their impression, I had learned my lesson. In the face of their esteem, which I could feel conjuring within me the false image of the perfect senior minister, I "turned sideways into the light and disappeared" before it. I refused to yield it any power, either in the search committee's mind or my own. Free of its allure, I reappeared before the committee as myself. The image of my highest self to which I bowed down was as the "senior minister who is loved by God and his congregation for who he really is, warts and all." The search committee responded even more energetically than before, moving mountains to bring me to Scottsdale. I gladly followed the call.

A month after my arrival, however, I experienced a direct challenge to my confidence that I had done the right thing. I was walking into the sanctuary on a Monday morning to collect some notes left at the pulpit the previous day. As I walked down the center aisle toward the chancel, a visual image passed before my mind's eye that stopped me dead in my tracks. The image was of *me*. I was lying on the steps leading up to the chancel. And I was crying. In fact, I was crying uncontrollably. The image appeared far more vivid and real than the casual images that normally drift through my head. I gasped and stood there, transfixed, wondering what it could mean.

"But you called me here to Scottsdale," I cried out to the empty sanctuary. "I know I messed up before, but you gave me a second chance! Remember? I learned my lesson! Please, please don't tell me I've messed it all up again!"

Still reeling from this experience, that very day I received a letter from a church in Michigan that was looking for a new minister. They acknowledged that I had only recently accepted the position in Scottsdale but said they would be interested in talking with me if things weren't working out as I had hoped. I thought to myself, "Is this a sign that I should leave before things head south on me here?"

I had to admit that the coincidence of receiving the letter on the very day I had been struck by such a potent vision (premonition?) seemed ominous. Still, I knew that the surest signs of the Spirit's whispers to the soul do not come through coincidental occurrences, no matter how unusual they may seem. Rather, they come through the lightning and thunder—those flashes of intuition whose ongoing reverberations elicit feelings of deep peace or quiet joy even if you are being called in a difficult direction. I had certainly felt zapped by lightning through the vision and the letter, but at the time I only felt reverberations of fear, and fear is *never* a trustworthy signal by which to set one's direction, particularly if it's the dominant signal.

I would need to do some significant soul-searching to determine which path of action was a response to fear and which produced a sense of flow. I spent time in my inner Dark Wood, envisioning staying in Scottsdale and also envisioning leaving. Every time I imagined leaving, feelings of fear, anger, and confusion welled up within me without so much as a whiff of joy or peace. When I envisioned staying in Scottsdale, peace welled up within me and my heart pounded happily, even though part of my consciousness was still disturbed by the vision and letter. I determined to stay.

As it happened, five years later I would in fact be crying like a baby on those very chancel steps in the Scottsdale sanctuary. Why was I crying? Before ending this story, let's pause and consider someone else's story. My story shares a lot in common with his. Taken together, both point to a similar response to that nagging question: *how does God respond when we falter and miss our call?*

DEAF, MUTE, AND FULL OF GRACE

The very first story in the Gospel of Luke is not about Jesus, but about a relative of Jesus named Zechariah, the priest who became the father of John the Baptist. I find Zechariah's story powerful not simply because it speaks of events leading up to the birth of John the Baptist and Jesus but because it speaks of events that *keep happening* up to our present day. In this respect, the story is full of mythological imagination. It attests to realities that were not simply "real long ago" but are "real all the time." Therefore, this story matters as much to us in our day as it did to the ancients.

According to the story, Zechariah is given what would likely have been a once-in-a-lifetime opportunity to stand in the Holy of Holies. The Holy of Holies was the most sacred spot in the Jewish Temple in Jerusalem. In fact, the Jews considered it the most sacred spot on earth. This was where the ark of the covenant was said to rest. The very presence of Yahweh was thought to be enthroned invisibly above the ark. So sacred was the Holy of Holies that it could only be entered once a year by a priest, chosen by lot, to tend the altar and its furnishings. To stand in the Holy of Holies would have been the poetic equivalent of standing before Patrick's Well in David Whyte's poem, only multiplied by several orders of magnitude.

> *Now you are alone with the transfiguration*
> *and ask no healing for your own*
> *but look down as if looking through time,*
> *as if through a rent veil from the other*
> *side of the question you've refused to ask.*

The Holy of Holies would have been considered a place so fully connected to God that standing inside it would offer a unique opportunity to receive your true name and identity. Apparently, Zechariah has some awareness of this. While the content of his prayer within the Holy of Holies is unknown, one may assume that Zechariah expects some particularly potent form of revelation there, perhaps a revelation of his destiny. Suddenly the archangel Gabriel stands before Zechariah saying, "Don't be afraid, Zechariah. Your prayers have been heard. Your wife Elizabeth will give birth to your son and you must name him John. He will be a joy and delight to you, and many people will rejoice at his birth, for he will be great in the Lord's eyes" (Luke 1:13-15).

Zechariah's identity is revealed: he will be known as the father of a child named John (that is, John the Baptist) through whom the world would receive a great and mighty blessing. Says the archangel, "He will be filled with the Holy Spirit even before his birth. He will bring many Israelites back to the Lord their God.... He will make ready a people prepared for the Lord" (Luke 1:15-17).

Knowing that his wife, Elizabeth, cannot bear children, Zechariah voices his doubts to the angel. Doubts?! Standing before one of Yahweh's highest angels in the Holy of Holies, Zechariah has doubts and dares to voice them: "How can I be sure of this? My wife and I are very old" (Luke 1:18). Even in the most sacred and powerful place on earth, Zechariah still can't seem to let go of the identity he'd entered with: childless. Whatever power had marked him with that name had marked him well.

In response, Gabriel announces that Zechariah will be mute until all is fulfilled. Apparently, Zechariah is also struck deaf, given what happens later.

Most interpreters of this story assume that Zechariah is being punished for his doubts. I don't see it this way. Who among us doesn't harbor doubts about our true identity? Our identity resides in the heart of our path, which is where we tap into incredible, nearly effortless energy. It's the place where body and soul converge with the Spirit in all its power. So when God reveals our proper name—our calling, mission, and identity that reflects our unique path—we *inevitably* struggle to accept it. We struggle because it appears as difficult to live *up to* as it is wonderful to live *into*. Why wouldn't it? Our pride tells us that we must live into this identity all by ourselves, under our own power and authority. On the other hand, our shame tells us we are unworthy of the calling to begin with—that it must be the product of wishful thinking. But the Spirit knows otherwise. In that special place where body, soul, and calling converge, the Spirit is able to offer our best help. If it is truly God calling and naming us, the question should no longer be, "How *can* I fulfill my identity and mission (by myself)," but, "How can I *not* fulfill it (with the help of the Spirit)?"

By striking Zechariah deaf and mute, God is not punishing him for failure to accept his true identity. God is *blessing* Zechariah, helping him accept that identity. How? Imagine how Zechariah's world might change over the coming nine months while Elizabeth is pregnant. He will be more of a silent observer of life than an active participant. The last sound Zechariah would have heard before his hearing was taken away was the sound of his son's name being spoken by the archangel Gabriel: "His name will be John." John is an abbreviated form of the Hebrew name Jonathan, which means "Yahweh [God] is gracious."

Can you imagine how your world might change if, for nine long months, you heard nothing, and said nothing, yet the last words you heard constantly ran through your head, "God is gracious"? Might you see your family, friends, and coworkers in a different light if the words "God is gracious" kept repeating themselves to you? Might you watch the evening news differently if you heard nothing but the words "God is gracious" as local, national, and world events flickered before you? Indeed, would the good, the bad, and the ugly of your own life appear any differently to you if it were marked by the words, "God is gracious, God is gracious, God is gracious"?

At the end of the story, Elizabeth gives birth to their miracle son. All their friends and relatives gather to hear what name he'll be given, expecting a conventional family name. When Elizabeth insists that he'll be named John, the crowd erupts in disapproval. "John's not a family name!" Finally, writing on a tablet, they ask Zechariah for his opinion on the matter. Using the tablet, Zechariah writes, "His name is John." Suddenly Zechariah's faculties return. He raises his voice high and loud in a hymn of praise, singing to the dumbfounded crowd of how special the child is, and what his special place will be in the world.

This story ends practically begging the question, *What is the miracle that gives you voice in the world? What treasure have you found in the darkness that blesses you and others?*

The story also ends with a note of irony that adds further nuance to our understanding of blessing and identity. This miracle child will indeed be a source of joy and blessing to Zechariah and Elizabeth as he lives into his calling as the forerunner of Jesus. Yet this same child will one day be imprisoned and beheaded by King Herod just for being who he was called to be. In this we are reminded that the Dark Wood's blessings never come without significant challenge. The presence of challenge and struggle, which many take as a sign that something is going wrong, may be a sign that something is going right. The story also reminds us that it is better to truly live before you die—by finding your path and finding your full humanity—than to die before you ever get around to living.

When Zechariah finally realized that God's graciousness was bound up with the everyday struggles, doubts, and uncertainties life had set before him, he became a Dark Wood wanderer. So it happens with any of us when we "turn sideways into the light and disappear" before any image of ourselves that is too small for us to live freely within. Some of these images are created by shame, which tell us that our struggles are the result of some intrinsic flaw for which God is punishing us. Other images are conjured by pride, which convinces us that our troubles are the result of God's inability to create the kind of world we would have for ourselves—a world that would never hurt or disappoint us.

When we finally accept the reality that God's grace and our struggles are inseparably bound together, we begin to understand the fierce wisdom behind the apostle Paul's striking insistence that "God works all things together for good for the ones who love God, for those who are called according to [God's] purpose" (Romans 8:28). Here, Paul does not claim that all things *are* good. Rather, he acknowledges that God is able to work all things *together* for good, provided we're willing to allow God's Spirit to guide our way through the darkness.

When we treat the Dark Wood as a place where the good, the bad, and the ugly in our lives can be embraced and explored rather than avoided, eventually we are able to look back over the path we've trod and make an affirmation that is unthinkable when sticking to the Adversary's broad streets of certainty and highways to success. We may say, "I never would have chosen to have X, Y, or Z happen, nor would I ever pass it off as 'good' or claim that it was 'all in God's plan.' Yet to stand in the place I now find myself, I would choose to live through it all over again." This is not an affirmation one makes easily or quickly or without due consideration of the very real pain and suffering one has experienced. Nor is it an affirmation one can make on behalf of others and their struggles. Still, it is an affirmation that Dark Wood wanderers are eventually able to make for themselves, wholeheartedly. They do so because they have discovered that an *Unexpected Love* meets them in darkness, and that struggle and grace have provided the light they needed to find their way forward.

BACK IN SCOTTSDALE

In the five years following my horrifying vision of crying on the chancel steps in the sanctuary of Scottsdale Congregational Church, I threw myself passionately into my work. I ruffled feathers. I challenged conventions. And I fell head over heels in love with my congregation. Those years weren't without challenge—at times, fierce struggle—but nearly every one kept pollinating our flower, blessing us and the world a little more.

Our sleepy little church transformed into a thriving hive of energy and activity, attracting scores of people who never thought they'd be caught dead in a Christian church. Serving my Scottsdale church so fully resonated with my sense of place in this world, tapping into my fullest energies and power, that I would have sooner died than move on.

So why did I find myself crying one day on the chancel steps, exactly as I'd seen in the vision five years earlier? One day as I walked into the sanctuary I simply couldn't get over the feeling of being so abundantly blessed to serve my Scottsdale congregation. Tears started flowing faster than I could control. I dropped to my knees and then lay fully upon the steps, I was so overcome with gratitude. I was crying tears *of joy*, not regret! There on the steps I suddenly remembered the vision I'd long forgotten, and the horrific interpretation I'd given it...and burst out laughing. The next five years turned out to be even better than the first five.

The ironic addendum to my story of missing my call to serve a church in Omaha is that I now, in fact, serve a church in Omaha, Nebraska. Only not the one I spoke of earlier. Countryside Community Church is a congregation a few miles down the road. After thirteen glorious years in Scottsdale, the lightning revealed that it was time to move to a new stage on the journey. While the decision to leave Scottsdale was incredibly difficult, it was also one of the more joyous decisions Melanie and I have ever made, as the draw to follow our new path was so pronounced. We had always expected that my next call after Scottsdale would be to serve a congregation in our native Pacific Northwest, a place we'd always longed to return to. Omaha was not even under consideration. But when Countryside began a conversation with me about being their next senior minister, the electrical storm raged once again, and we readily followed. I guess the Spirit had reasons for bringing us to Omaha one way or another!

Bottom line, God does not punish us for making mistakes. Even when we allow ourselves to be marked by a name that's too small for us, veering sharply off course as a result, the Spirit keeps uttering our true name and seems to know plenty of alternate paths that will allow us to live into it. Of course, mistakes do not come without pain. But mistakes made while trying to be *ourselves*, not someone else, bring us closer to our place in this world, not farther from it. It is perhaps through our mistakes more than anything else that we learn to "turn sideways into the light and disappear" before any life that cannot be lived in freedom. We rediscover who we are and whose we are, only to reappear in the world with new vision and confidence, and with a new name: child of God.

8

THE GIFT OF MISFITS

The world is so empty if one thinks only of mountains,
rivers & cities;
but to know someone who thinks and feels with us,
and who, though distant,
is close to us in spirit, this makes the earth for us
an inhabited garden.
—Johann Wolfgang von Goethe

THE VERY FIRST WORDS OUT OF Jesus' mouth during his public ministry were so controversial that his audience struggled hard to accept them. It can reasonably be argued that this message more than any other was responsible for Jesus' death. According to the Gospel of Matthew, Jesus' message was this: *"Change your whole way of thinking! Heaven is already here!"* (Matthew 4:17, author's translation). If this is the first time you have heard Jesus' message put this way, you are not alone. Most of us hear the following version on the lips of every angry street preacher: *"Repent, for the kingdom of heaven has come near"* (Matthew 4:17 NRSV).

Both versions of Jesus' message are faithful to the underlying Greek.[1] Yet why do we only ever encounter the latter version (or minor variants) in our Bibles and in preachers' sermons, especially when the implications are so profoundly different? The first version sounds like Jesus is offering us an opportunity: "If you're waiting to go to heaven, wait no longer. Change your whole way of thinking and you'll discover that heaven has been waiting for you all along!" To these words the Gospel of Mark adds, "Believe in the *good news!*" (1:15 NRSV, emphasis added).

The second version sounds like Jesus is issuing a threat: "You'd better confess your sins and believe in me before it's too late! God's coming soon and will either condemn you to eternal torture in hell or invite you into paradise depending on how you respond right now!"

Of course, it's a lot easier to fill church pews—and coffers—with the second version, especially since people tend to add so many extra things to it like I just did. Yet there may be another reason the second translation receives greater play besides greed and power. While the first version is more invitational and positive, it's also a lot harder to accept at face value. After all, if heaven is not just an afterlife experience but is here and available right now, then why is the world so messed up?

I can hear Jesus' ancient audience responding with cynicism. "Are you insane, Jesus? How can heaven be here when the Romans are on our backs, oppressing our people and taxing us into poverty?" Another responds, "How can heaven be now when my father just died?" Still another asks, "How can heaven be here when there is so much oppression and so little justice?"

Curiously, what Jesus says next strongly suggests that the more invitational translation is truer to Jesus' original intent than the traditional one. For Jesus' very next words of teaching in Matthew's Gospel are best understood as a rebuttal to the very objections a cynical audience would raise to the claim that our experience of "heaven" has already begun (Matthew 5:3-12). In his famous Beatitudes or "blessed be" statements, Jesus offers examples of people who find deep blessing in this world, including those who:

- are poor in spirit
- mourn the loss of a loved one
- hunger and thirst for righteousness (which is absent)
- make peace in the midst of conflict
- are persecuted
- are slandered and discredited

On and on Jesus goes, overturning his audience's view of heaven and offering some shocking "implications" as a result. These include the need to love our enemies, to pray for our persecutors, and to acknowledge that God "makes the sun rise both on the evil and the good and sends rain on both the righteous and the unrighteous" (Matthew 5:45).

If heaven, or "God's kingdom" as Mark puts it, is really here and available right now—perhaps not in its fullness but in some significant, meaningful way—then we do indeed need to change our whole way of thinking to believe the good news. Heaven must be messy. For one basic fact about our world is that it is a place of constant struggle. If heaven may be found here and now, then heaven cannot be merely found in the *absence* of struggle as most of us assume, but *in the very heart of our struggles*. If Jesus' message is true, then our deepest challenges may offer our most profound opportunities. Heaven is found in the Dark Wood!

Thankfully, none of us make this journey alone. Up to this point in our exploration of the Dark Wood, we've been considering the quest for our life's path primarily from the perspective of our journey as individuals. It is only as individuals that we awaken to find ourselves in the Dark Wood, and each of us must find our own distinctive path through it. Yet, given the difficulties and challenges we encounter in the Dark Wood, walking alone is about as advisable as walking alone in a physical dark wood. It's easy to get lost without the aid of companions. And it is often through them that we receive our clearest glimpses of heaven.

This "both/and" nature of our experience of the Dark Wood as individuals and in community is given curious expression in one of Jesus' most famous statements about the kingdom of God. When grilled by some Pharisees who had a hard time swallowing his claim about the immediacy of heaven they asked Jesus when they would finally be able to see it for themselves. He replied in exasperation,

> *The kingdom of God is* within *you.*
> *(Luke 17:21 NRSV, emphasis added)*
>
> *The kingdom of God is already* among *you.*
> *(Luke 17:21, emphasis added)*

These two quotes are not separate statements but are different translations of the same sentence in the Greek New Testament. The difference lies in how the Greek word, *entos*, is rendered. *Entos* means "within." But it can mean either "within," as in "within your soul," or it can mean "within" as in "in the midst of you" or "among you." So is the kingdom of God found, entered, and lived *within* the individual or *among* the community? Once again, we might hear Rabbi Eliezar answering, "Yes!"

As Buddhists know well, this is the rationale for emphasizing the value of the *Sangha*, or community dedicated to practicing "the good way, the upright way, the knowledgeable way, and the proper way."[2] While we all walk our paths as individuals, the lone seeker is more likely to get lost or to give up than the one who travels in company.

Granted, the Spirit sends every individual plenty of lightning and thunder to be of guidance, but none of us are perfect interpreters of these signals. We make mistakes. Other times we lack the courage to go forward. And, like Zechariah the priest, most of us have a difficult time letting go of that old familiar image of the false self that keeps trying to mark us with too small a name, even as the storm of our true identity rages all around us. Making the journey with a few wise companions by your side can keep you from getting lost and make the journey less lonely, even fun. Fun especially when we discover that we may also be of help to our companions as they strive to find their place in the world.

The importance of traveling with companions becomes more pronounced when you consider what forces you're up against if you try to make the journey on your own. If your goal is to wander the Dark Wood alone, waiting for its storms to guide you, following where the lightning and thunder indicates, you might do just fine provided there is no interference from other sources. But the unfortunate reality is that life tends to get in the way of our best intentions. We go to work, we turn on the television, we get sick, we argue with a loved one. The world impacts our lived experience in any number of ways each day, and not all these impacts are necessarily supportive of walking the spiritual path. *Did the ancients know any of this?* you may wonder. "Be clearheaded. Keep alert. Your [Adversary], the devil, is on the prowl like a roaring lion, seeking someone to devour" (1 Peter 5:8).

MAC-N-CHEESE

In the early 1990s, my wife, Melanie, worked as a food technologist in Research and Development for a national frozen foods manufacturer. One of her team's projects involved developing a new macaroni and cheese product for the frozen food aisle of supermarkets.

The team worked hard and brilliantly. To this day, Melanie has not shared with me the secrets of what the team did to make their prototype macaroni and cheese so good. I can imagine them searching for special cheeses that would retain their distinct aromas and textures after being frozen and reheated. Perhaps they experimented with various ingredients and extracts that would bring together the flavors of two or more cheeses and give the dish a rich and creamy "mouth feel" without seeming heavy or overly filling. I can see them trying out various forms of macaroni to ensure it would retain an al dente springiness after being zapped in a microwave oven. What my wife *will* divulge is that, after all this work, the product they developed was, hands down, better than any version you could find in the market at the time. In fact, it was better than homemade! The coup de grâce for the manufacturer was that its cost of production was within their target range.

Before going into production, however, the product had to be tested to ensure it was a right match for consumers. Management knew there is often a difference between what tastes good and what sells. The marketing department invited a group of consumers who represented the general population into their facility to sample the new macaroni and cheese. The result?

Those who identified themselves as cheese lovers said they loved it and were ready to buy. By the truckload. Those who identified themselves as *not* liking cheese had a different opinion altogether. They weren't the slightest bit interested in purchasing the product. Then there were those who identified themselves as indifferent to cheese. They said the product tasted a bit too cheesy, but they might purchase it on a good coupon special.

As a result of this consumer feedback, the manufacturer decided to send the food technologists back to their test kitchen, instructing them to develop an alternate, less cheesy version. Then, they brought back the consumer focus group to test the new product.

This time, the cheese lovers were greatly disappointed, but

when push came to shove they admitted that they'd probably purchase the product anyway. While it didn't taste nearly as cheesy as before, it at least *hinted* at cheese, and they sure loved cheese. Those who were indifferent to cheese thought it was a winner. To them, it tasted like cheese, but didn't taste *much* like cheese, so they'd readily purchase it. Even the cheese haters acknowledged that they would make a purchase. After all, other people in their household liked cheese, and if they *had* to eat some, this would be their product of choice.

You can guess which product made it to a frozen food aisle near you. The triumph of the mediocre.

As mentioned earlier, I am a foodie. Although it is tempting, it would be unfair to excoriate the manufacturer for developing a bland, frozen macaroni-and-cheese product. Why should the people who are indifferent to, or hate, cheese be forced to eat the cheesiest version of macaroni and cheese that can possibly be produced? In a food industry dominated by the economies of mass production, sales, and consumption, it is probably fairer—and certainly more profitable—to make something that appeals to a broader audience than to just the few who would go to the moon to find a good piece of cheese, especially if you can bring the cheese lovers along for the ride.

But what if you are a cheese lover who doesn't want to go along for the ride? And what if it's not macaroni and cheese you're interested in but finding your distinctive path through life? Now things get complicated.

When it comes to finding your place in the world, your central challenge looks like this: Imagine that you are asked to sit down at a table and a box of frozen macaroni and cheese is placed before you. Now imagine that the one who sat you there assumes that there is not a shred of difference between you and the frozen food product.

Of course, it would be a stretch to assume that people actually treat others this way. *People* don't often do this. But *processes* do. Countless are the *processes* that seek to tame the wild energy inside you, just as they seek to tame the wild energies of the world. While this energy inside you is a direct gift from the Spirit, there are a number of processes governing everything about you, from your vocation to your vacation, that will attempt to shape your life until it is as palatable to the masses as that macaroni and cheese product. These cultural and economic processes start working on you early in life, long before you become aware of what is even happening. Far better *to consume you* this way.

These *processes* that treat you as if you were nothing more than raw material on a production line are enormously powerful features of the culture we live in. Like fish in the ocean, we largely move through life unaware of the social, cultural, and economic waters we swim in because we are so thoroughly immersed in them. If you live an unreflective life, allowing these forces to shape you unawares, they will take away your name and give you a number. They will not ask what brings you alive in this world, but will demand instead that their world lives in you. They will not ask what is the *specific* good that you must do to live into your full humanity. Instead they will empower you to do only the good that keeps their specific processes alive and well, running seven days a week, twenty-four hours a day.

To be sure, the powers behind these processes will work hard to make you happy to do these "good" things. They will reward you financially, or at least promise financial gain. They will create endless amounts of entertainment that will shape your desires in such a way that *their values* become *your ideals.* They'll shape business, politics, education, even the arts and religion, to support these values and they will make you feel "righteous" or "patriotic" for supporting them, too. Then they will *own* you. Your life will serve the lowest common denominator, whose only "high" comes from drinking the cheap beer of the Adversary.

We don't think about all this most of the time. At least we don't until we either get a taste of the sublime and begin to dream about what life *could* be like, or we fall into despair and wonder how life has drifted so far from anything we love or care about. Then we start to pine for the Dark Wood where strange gifts like *uncertainty, getting lost,* and *being thunderstruck* hold more promise than the certain drudgery we experience on a plain, clear path straight to nowhere.

If we enter the Dark Wood alone, and stay there alone, the odds are stacked against us that we will be back at the Adversary's taverns in no time, drinking and worshiping at the Cult of the Mediocre. The Spirit knows this, which is why the Dark Wood offers another gift, one that may be the most important of all. I call this gift the community of fellow misfits.

You may react to the word *misfit,* reading into it more than I intend. What I mean by *misfit* is someone who is being as intentional as you are about embracing the gifts of the Dark Wood and finding their place in this world, if not more so. These are comparatively rare individuals in a world absorbed by materialism, mass-market consumerism, "religitainment," and quick fixes. Yet there are more than enough of these misfits who swim against the current to find a small community even in the smallest of towns. If you're not aware of them, you haven't been looking, or you have been too certain that you cannot find them to send out any signals that you are interested in their company. There are at least three types of misfits who may serve as powerful companions in our travels in the Dark Wood.

MISFIT #1

The first misfit is an interpretive guide or mentor. This is a person who has spent a little longer in the Dark Wood than you have and is therefore more familiar with trails that lead to dead ends, or over cliffs, or back out into the bright and broad streets that lead straight toward doing the wrong good. This guide isn't always at your side, but is a wise person you can check in with regularly, particularly when the trail becomes faint or the wait between lightning flashes is long. My mentor and I check in with each other every month.

A mentor may be someone whose life's path closely matches your own, but not always. It is more important to find someone familiar with the Dark Wood, regardless of what brings them alive in the world. The person might be a spiritual director or clergyperson, a professional counselor, or simply a wise old friend. To draw on the food analogy, a mentor is someone who can say, "Forget the frozen stuff. Let's make a batch of homemade mac-n-cheese. We'll add a bit of this and that until it makes our taste buds perk up and cry, 'More!'"

A wise mentor with deep experience in the Dark Wood of life, whom you trust implicitly, who listens without judging and shares perspectives freely without trying to turn you into a miniature version of themselves, is invaluable. Like a loving spouse, they are worth keeping for a lifetime and worth seeking out if you don't have one. Thanks to modern communication technologies it is now possible to establish a mentoring relationship long-distance, even between people who have never met face-to-face. More important, modern communication technology makes it possible to maintain a mentoring relationship for many years, even a lifetime.

I have had the same mentor for the last thirty-four years. This is my friend Bruce, whom you met in chapters 3 and 7. Yet we have lived in close proximity to each other just four of those years.

What this mentoring relationship has done for me over time is allow me to explore far more of the Dark Wood and its gifts than I ever could have otherwise. Frequently, it has been Bruce who has perceived a beautiful gift waiting to be claimed within a difficult situation that I may have missed entirely. He has also spotted serious pitfalls lying within what appeared to be grand opportunities. Over the years I have been able to offer him a helpful perspective or two as well. Naturally, Bruce has become a good friend and confidant. Our relationship has made me a better husband, father, minister, writer, and friend. It has also drawn me closer to God and made me a more sensitive and faithful listener to the Spirit.

Besides flesh-and-blood mentors, books may also serve a mentoring role to a limited extent. They bring us together with wise people who may advise us even when there is no way to be physically present with them and no way to establish contact remotely. Every great faith tradition, for instance, has its ancient mythologies and sacred texts written by people who know the Dark Wood well and speak from lengthy experience in this territory. I find the Jewish and Christian Scriptures helpful in this regard—when taken metaphorically and free from any notion of inerrancy. I also find the writings of Rūmī, whom I mentioned in chapter 3, to be of help, as are the writings of the ancient Christian mystics cited in the first chapter.

Contemporary books, too, can help translate the wisdom of the ages into a modern idiom. But books can only get you so far. After all, the authors do not typically know you personally, nor you them. A book is not the same as a living, breathing person who knows your story, who may love you (or at least like or respect you), who can give advice in real time under changing conditions.

MISFIT #2

The second misfit aid to our journey through the Dark Wood is a small band of travelling companions. They do not have to be as familiar with the Dark Wood as your mentor, nor need they be on the same path as you. They simply need to be committed to finding and living within their own place of aliveness, following their own sense of call that keeps them from worshiping at the shrines of the mediocre. In Quakerism, they call this a "society of friends."

These companions will likely be, or eventually become, close friends. While friendship may not be an aspect of the relationship at first (it takes time), this aspect is critical. Critical because you check in with these companions more frequently than with your mentor. And whether they are fellow professionals or simply friends on a journey together, these are people with whom you can let your hair down and simply be yourself. They are the folks to whom you can reveal your triumphs and tragedies, your joys and fears, and they to you. You come to their aid when they are down, and they do the same for you. Following the food analogy, these companions are your spiritual "gourmet group." What brings them together is their love of great food. What *keeps* them together is their love for each other. In this sense, they are like welcoming campfires in the Dark Wood, providing warmth and comfort as well as illumination. They value Dark Wood gifts like emptiness, uncertainty, being lost just as readily as they celebrate triumphs and achievements. It is from within such groups that you come to recognize a very important thing about yourself: that you are not alone.

My closest misfit companions meet once a week for two or more hours. Only two of us share the same profession but we all share a love of exploring the Dark Wood. Sometimes we study various topics of interest, perhaps supported by a book or DVD.

Mostly we study the Scriptures together, asking questions about their significance for our lives. Whatever we do, the point is not the doing but the being, as in being-in-relationship. The wisdom we seek seems to come more frequently when we are sharing deeply about our lives and engaged honestly with the Scriptures. Of course, we maintain strict confidentiality, which is the hallmark of any serious group of misfits exploring the Dark Wood.

While I find that a small group that meets regularly is by far the most helpful, I also travel the Dark Wood with a group of seven misfit companions who are separated by great distances and therefore meet just once a year. Members of this group all share the same profession (they're all renegade clergy), yet we are not united simply by profession but by our commitment to uniting the spiritual and vocational path, developing this path to the best of our abilities. Curiously, such groups are unusual even among ministers. They are a rare breed in any profession. Thus, geographic proximity is not a luxury they often share.

Of course, these groups require a serious investment of time and money to meet physically each year, though the group I belong to cuts costs by finding free accommodations and preparing meals together. We find that the cumulative wisdom shared among the group regarding our specific calling, as well as the robust camaraderie, far outweighs the investment. I get more mileage out of my investment in this small, intimate group of misfit colleagues than I do at a handful of conferences featuring a laundry list of noted speakers. (Thus, you will not find me at many conferences unless I'm speaking at them.)

MISFIT #3

The third misfit gift of the Dark Wood is a bit different from the others. It's rarer and therefore harder to find. As with any rare object, there are plenty of cheap imitations hawked by street vendors to the unsuspecting deal hunter. Because there are so many cheap imitations of this particular gift, it is hard to speak of this gift directly. Most people are only familiar with the knockoffs and thus would not view this gift as anything special. The third misfit gift of the Dark Wood is a community of faith—not just any community, but a misfit community of faith.

Just as individuals have distinctive paths or callings, so do communities. Currently there are a number of misfit communities that I see rising from the ashes of the world's dead and dying religious traditions. These particular communities have found, or are in the process of finding, an identity that looks quite different from their predecessors. If a personal mentor could be likened to an interpretive guide in the Dark Wood, and a small group of Dark Wood traveling companions could be likened to a group around a campfire, a misfit community of faith could be likened to an alehouse in the Dark Wood. As is common at alehouses in Great Britain or Ireland, those who gather in these misfit faith communities are drawn there for camaraderie and conversation, as well as the basic spirit of the place—which in both venues may be more the product of the Holy Spirit's work than one might think. At times, the whole place may break out singing—or fighting! They cater to a diverse crowd. Yet there is a spirit within them that transcends differences and gives each its distinctive identity. Just as no two alehouses are alike, neither are these misfit faith communities.

In my experience, these faith communities may be associated with a particular denomination or religious tradition, they normally exist on the fringes of them. Still others are not associated with any particular institution or single faith tradition. No small number take the form of house gatherings, many of which meet in rural areas where few choices exist if one does not resonate with more orthodox interpretations of faith. Some of these communities even meet in bars or brew pubs—making the alehouse analogy all the more appropriate! While I lead a large church in Omaha, I also have been part of a group that meets in a bar downtown and with another group that meets weekly in a coffeehouse and calls itself Darkwood Brew.[3]

All these fringe, sometimes experimental, communities are part of something very interesting and mysterious happening now at the grassroots, not just in the United States but globally, and not just in any one faith tradition. In the eyes of many, the old orthodoxies of the classic world religions, which centuries ago provided light and life to the faithful, have drifted far from the primal "fire" that gave them birth. The classic orthodoxies have become stale and rigid, fleeing from mystery and uncertainty, promoting a one-size-fits-all path to spiritual or worldly "success" and showing precious little tolerance of difference or appreciation for diversity. They are crumbling. In their place, a "heady heterodoxy" of sorts is forming. A sizeable band of misfits.

To label these fringe communities *heterodox* (that is, at variance with established belief) or *misfit* does not mean that they have abandoned their native traditions. Rather, in the history of world religions, the heterodox tend to reflect the growing edge, or widening circle, of a particular faith. In time, what is considered fringe or heterodox becomes increasingly accepted, later becoming a "new center" of a new orthodoxy (which eventually will give rise to a new heterodoxy which will morph into a new orthodoxy, and so it goes). While the old orthodoxies tend to view the heterodox as a threat to their faith, history shows that this is rarely the case. While these new misfit communities are challenging certain aspects of the old orthodoxies, they are not throwing out the ancient tradition but deeply honoring it by moving the tradition forward in light of fresh insight from the Holy Spirit, which continues to speak in our world. As author and fellow Dark Wood traveler Brian McLaren observes, these communities are establishing a more "generous orthodoxy."[4]

What is particularly intriguing about this development is that as these communities respond to the Holy Spirit they are discovering a substantial foundation of common ground between adherents of many faiths. For instance, certain Jewish, Christian, and Muslim communities are discovering that they share more in common with one another than with the orthodox strands of their own traditions. Even though the framing beliefs of these emerging and converging communities remain distinct from one another, their core values are looking increasingly similar. While members of these communities claim to feel more Christian, Muslim, or Jewish than ever, they are also looking more like one another than ever before. They show strong evidence of responding to the same Spirit, who is fostering similar core values within the differing beliefs that frame those values.[5]

What follows are twelve characteristics that, in my experience, constitute the new foundation of common ground. They are part of the new identity toward which these communities are moving, while retaining beliefs and practices that are distinctive to their particular traditions. These characteristics fall under three general categories that some call *the three great loves*: love of God, love of neighbor, and love of self. For each characteristic, I have identified something these heterodox communities generally are letting go of (making them heterodox), and the new revelation they generally are embracing. By saying *generally*, I mean that not all communities are exactly alike. Some share more of this common ground than others. I believe the time is coming when these twelve attributes will be part of what is considered the new "center" by adherents of many faiths.

LOVE OF GOD

1. They are letting go of the notion that their particular faith is the only legitimate one on the planet. They are embracing an understanding that God is greater than our imagination can comprehend (or fence in), and thus they are open to the possibility that God may speak within and across all faith traditions.

2. They are letting go of literal and inerrant interpretations of their sacred Scriptures while celebrating the unique treasures

that their Scriptures contain. They are embracing a more ancient, prayerful, metaphorical approach to these same Scriptures, finding new insights and resources as they explore the mythological imagination at work in them.

3. They are letting go of the notion that people of faith are called to dominate nature. They are embracing a more organic understanding of human relationship with the earth.

4. They are letting go of empty worship conventions and an overemphasis on doctrines as tools of division and exclusion. They are embracing more diverse, creative, engaging approaches, often making strong use of the arts.

LOVE OF NEIGHBOR

5. They are letting go of racial prejudice and a narrow definition of sexual orientation and gender identity. They are embracing with increasing confidence an understanding that affirms the dignity and worth of all people.

6. They are letting go of an understanding that people of faith should only interest themselves in the spiritual well-being of people. They are embracing a more holistic understanding that physical and spiritual well-being are related.

7. They are letting go of the desire to impose their particular vision of faith on wider society. They are embracing the notion that their purpose is to make *themselves* more faithful adherents of their vision of faith.

8. They are letting go of the old rivalries between "liberal,

moderate, and conservative" branches of their faith. They are embracing a faith that transcends these very definitions.

LOVE OF SELF

9. They are letting go of notions of the afterlife that are dominated by judgment of "unbelievers." They are embracing an understanding that, as God's creations, God is eternally faithful to us, and that all people are loved far more than we can comprehend.

10. They are letting go of the notion that faith and science are incompatible. They are embracing the notion that faith and science can serve as allies in the pursuit of truth, and that God values our minds as well as our hearts.

11. They are letting go of the notion that one's work and one's spiritual path are unrelated. They are embracing an understanding that rest and recreation, prayer and reflection, are as important as work, and that our work is a calling and expression of our sweet spot.

12. They are letting go of old hierarchies that privilege religious leaders over laypeople. They are embracing an understanding that all people have a mission and purpose in life in response to the call of the Holy Spirit. It's no longer about who wears the robes but who lives the life.

Indeed, when you witness what is happening in these emerging and converging communities—happening around the world and often without knowledge of similar trends in other communities—one thing becomes clear: while, in certain circumstances, the major faith traditions of the world may have let go of the awe, wonder, and wild joy of the Spirit, the Spirit has not let go of them. God continues to flash and thunder; liquid joy continues to rain upon us. People are making their way into the Dark Wood. There they are finding a sense of wholeheartedness that comes when body, soul, and the call of the Spirit converge. Some call this convergence point their place in this world. Others call it the kingdom of God.

9

WHERE WE GO FROM HERE

I tell you that you are Peter. And I'll build my church on this
rock. The gates of the underworld won't be able to stand
against it.
—Jesus, renaming Simon (Matthew 16:18)

IN THE FIRST CHAPTER WE OBSERVED that the Rock upon which
Jesus said he would build his church was never intended to be the
firm foundation most people assume. The "Rock" Jesus referred to
was Simon, whom Jesus had renamed Peter ("Rock") after *sinking*
like a rock in the Sea of Galilee. If Peter's attempt to walk on water signals the character of the community Jesus sought to build,
then it would most certainly be adventurous, daring, responsive to
Jesus' call...and somewhat prone to failure. One might even sur-
mise that Jesus considered *right failure* to be at least as important
as *right belief* or *right action*.

Unfortunately, much of the modern community of Jesus
seems to have lost sight of all this. Many are terrified of failure,

believing it to be a sign of unfaithfulness and God's displeasure, not the foundation of the church Jesus sought to establish. Rather than placing their faith in a *sinking* Rock, many churches promote an image of lasting success that their followers can supposedly attain through the foundation of *right belief*—belief defined by whomever happens to represent their ideal image of success at the time. When *right belief* fails to yield the results they desire, churches turn to *right action* as the antidote. Depending on the flavor of their particular theology, churches promote morality agendas or social justice campaigns or simply turn to self-help programs that promise to reveal the road to success in "seven easy steps." In so doing, these churches remove themselves from the lived experience of their participants. In everyday life, the steps are never so easy, and path to morality and justice is never as straight, clear, or unencumbered as we are led to believe.

Embracing our propensity for failure might seem negative to someone unfamiliar with the Dark Wood. Yet by now you have probably begun to sense that the experiences you try so hard to avoid hold the potential to bless you with unexpected gifts if you allow them. When you embrace time spent in the Dark Wood rather than seeking to run away at the first opportunity, you discover that you are connected to a Higher Power—one who offers important clues about who you are and what you're here for. You also develop the confidence and determination necessary to hold tight to these realities rather than letting go of them at the first sign of trouble. Together we have explored the vast implications of this counterintuitive reality of life in the Dark Wood, chief among them being that you don't have to be a saint to find your place in this world. All you really need to be *is struggling.*

As I mentioned in the first chapter, one of my greatest childhood heroes was Peter. I used to be amazed that Peter could play such a central role among Jesus' disciples and in the early church despite his many flaws. In light of my adult awareness of the Dark Wood, I have come to realize that Peter's accomplishments did not happen *despite* his shortcomings and failures but *in and through them.* Peter was a Dark Wood wanderer. He was intimately familiar with experiences of emptiness, uncertainty, and temptation that open us up to the Spirit's guidance and clarify our next steps. Peter was well acquainted with getting lost, being thunderstruck, and disappearing before images of life, self, and God that were too small for him—often through hard experience. Each of these taught Peter something about following a God who confounds our greatest certainties and takes us on a journey that is anything but linear; who challenges us to live into the highest vision of ourselves, not the lowest; who calls us into community with others who reflect these same values.

Nowhere were the gifts Peter received in the Dark Wood more helpful than when he was confronted with his life's greatest challenge. This challenge would result in Peter's greatest lasting achievement as well, proving Jesus' intuition that a sinking Rock would provide the surest foundation of the community that would later gather in his name. You may find that this final story of Peter's journey through the Dark Wood embraces your own story in surprising ways, confirming the gifts that may be found within your own struggles.

Few of us realize that the greatest argument in the first century among Christians was over the inclusion of non-Jewish Gentiles in the church. Jesus' first followers were Jewish, not Gentile. They did not call themselves "Christian" but simply followers of "The Way" who believed that Jesus was the Messiah predicted in the Hebrew Scriptures (Acts 9:2). They observed the levitical dietary codes, practiced circumcision, studied the Torah, and strove to follow the strictures of Mosaic law as fervently as any other Jewish community.

In Peter's day, large numbers of Gentiles yearned to join the Jewish community but were prevented by Jewish law from doing so. These Gentiles were called "God-fearers."[1] "God-fearers" were philosophically attracted to Jewish monotheism, yet because they were not circumcised and did not follow Jewish dietary restrictions, they could only go so far within Judaism. Their financial donations were certainly accepted by synagogues, some of which received the majority of their revenue from Gentile God-fearers, yet they were not allowed to worship in the sanctuary like the rest. Instead, God-fearers were corralled into a special courtyard outside the sanctuary, separated from the "true believers," straining to overhear what was going on inside.

When a new sect arose within Judaism—the early Jesus followers—some of these God-fearers naturally wanted to learn more about it. Certainly, many wanted to learn about Jesus. Yet just as certainly they wanted to know if this new sect would allow them full inclusion into the life of the community. Until Peter and a curious vision he had while at prayer on a rooftop, the answer to this question was categorically no! Since most Christians in the modern era are non-Jewish Gentiles, it hardly crosses their minds that the church would ever struggle over the issue of their inclusion. But struggle they most certainly did!

PETER'S PICKLE

In the tenth chapter of the book of Acts, we find Peter praying on the rooftop of a home in the village of Joppa, on the coast of Israel near the modern city of Tel Aviv. After some time, Peter gets hungry and his thoughts drift toward lunch. Yet rather than ending his prayer and eating like most of us would, Peter asks for lunch to be prepared and brought to him as he continues on. Then comes a vision: something like a blanket drifts down from the sky suspended by ropes. On this blanket are all kinds of animals that Jewish law considers "unclean" (non-kosher) and therefore forbidden to consume. A voice says, "Get up, Peter; kill and eat" (v. 13 NRSV).

Shocked by the invitation to consume contraband meat, Peter refuses, saying essentially, "That isn't *kosher!*"

The voice responds, "What God has made clean, you must not call profane" (v. 15 NRSV).

Curiously, Peter and his Jewish ancestors have refused to eat non-kosher animals for a thousand years precisely because they believed God had pronounced them "unclean" and labeled their consumption an *abomination!* Their restrictive diet was an outgrowth of their love, devotion, and humble obedience to God's law. Peter knew that the book of Leviticus clearly states, for instance, that camels are unclean because they chew the cud and don't have a divided hoof. Cows are clean because they chew the cud and *do* have a divided hoof. Fish with scales are fine to eat, but scallops, oysters, and crabs are unclean because they live in the sea and don't have fins or scales. Peter had been taught these things since he was a child. Before Peter's vision came, if someone had told him that eating kosher wasn't required anymore, he probably would have accused them of arrogance or apostasy or both.

Despite the objections Peter raised, he kept praying concerning the vision. As he prayed, Peter probably tried to assess where the vision was coming from. Was it the Holy Spirit or his stomach talking? While the book of Acts makes the origin of the vision clear—it is indeed from the Holy Spirit—we must not assume it was so clear to Peter, at least initially. As we observed in chapter 4, the Holy Spirit does not speak audibly to people, even to heroes of the Bible. The Spirit often speaks through "thunder and lightning"—those flashes of intuition, "aha" experiences, and sweet-spot moments that give us a glimpse of something higher.

One of the signs that we are hearing the Spirit's call is that it doesn't come just once, but keeps reverberating within us like echoing thunder. It's like a voice deep inside keeps crying, "Home!" whenever we entertain a certain thought or direction. We yearn to follow in the direction of this voice just as a rubber ball held underwater strains to be set free to rise to the surface. Yet when we are being called to take a significant risk, we are also called to apply a higher degree of skepticism and discernment. We must test the vision more fully before running with it. When Peter's vision of the blanket full of contraband meat returned a second time, he still was not ready to accept the Spirit's invitation. As alluring as it may have been, the vision represented too great a break from his tradition to be accepted without significant challenge. So Peter pushed the vision away and continued to pray. Sure enough, the vision returned again. Just as Peter was puzzling over its third appearance, he was interrupted by an unexpected knock at the door.

Often, when we're willing to listen for the Holy Spirit yet are unsure of what the Spirit is trying to tell us (or are unsure of the source of the message), the Spirit approaches us from a new angle, using "vocabulary" that is more overt and insistent. While Peter is still praying, three Gentiles arrive requesting that Peter accompany them to Caesarea where a prominent Roman military commander—one of the God-fearers—yearns to explore what it means to follow Jesus.

Now Peter is *really* stretched. As if his vision of consuming unclean foods wasn't enough, now he is being asked to associate with *Gentiles*. Doubtless, Scripture starts running through Peter's head again. Memories from the book of Nehemiah float to the surface—memories of Jews divorcing their foreign wives in order to become purer in God's sight; memories of Jews being commanded not to associate with the Gentiles. The three Gentiles at the door represent the *worst* kind of Gentile, too—those associated with a military regime who have oppressed Israel for years and killed Peter's master, Jesus.

As these three Gentiles made their request to Peter, he was probably filled with myriad conflicting thoughts and emotions. His head was surely telling him one thing: "Don't do it! This is apostasy! This is an *abomination*." Yet if the vision of the blanket and simultaneous appearance of three Gentiles were the Holy Spirit's work, as the book of Acts portrays them to be, then Peter was almost certainly experiencing a series of significant sweet-spot moments—intuitive cascades of "liquid joy"—whenever he considered eating the contraband food or accepting the Gentiles' invitation. In fact, the similarity between the feelings provoked by each set of thoughts probably helped Peter connect the dots between the two. The message the Spirit was trying to evoke within him was not just about accepting "unclean" *food*, but "unclean" *people*. The Spirit was calling Peter to remove the barriers that kept Gentile God-fearers from full participation in the early Christian community.

If Peter were a modern-day Christian, he likely would have ignored his gut intuitions altogether and assumed that God's thoughts on the subject of non-kosher food and non-Jewish people had been permanently established in Scripture. He might have quoted the bumper sticker that reads, "God wrote it. I believe it. That settles it!" He may have stood upon a stack of Bibles insisting that the Word of God plainly and clearly indicates in black-and-white that both the vision and the invitation of the Gentiles at his door were nothing less than temptations sent by the Adversary to engage in behavior that God considers an *abomination*. Ironically, had Peter taken this modern Christian approach and his community followed suit, most modern-day Christians would be refused entry inside Christian churches!

But Peter did not do any of the things a modern-day Christian might do. Why? In part, because Peter wasn't a modern-day

Christian. Peter didn't hold the same assumptions about Scripture that many do in our day. His Bible, like that of Jesus, was the Hebrew Scriptures. (The Christian New Testament would not be produced for another three centuries.) While Peter listened for God's word in Scripture, he apparently assumed that Scripture's purpose was not to replace direct experience of the Holy Spirit. Rather, its purpose is to *set us into relationship with the Spirit* whose call frequently challenges our most cherished assumptions—sometimes even assumptions created by Scripture itself.

When the three Gentiles appeared at his door, and Peter connected the dots between their appearance and his threefold vision, Peter became convinced that the Holy Spirit was calling him to remove the barriers between them. In taking a step toward Caesarea, Peter stepped away not only from his house in Joppa but from the figurative boat of his tradition—from nearly a thousand years of faith and practice—and set foot once again on the stormy sea of uncertainty. Only this time he was less afraid than the first. Peter knew it was safe to take a risk—even a large one—if he sensed the Spirit calling him do so. He had learned firsthand that when you follow your deepest sense of call, you do not step out onto that sea alone. If you lose your nerve and sink when following the Spirit's call, you need only reach up for help. You will discover yourself grasped by a power that is not ready to let go of you.

So Peter steps out onto that sea more calmly than before, heading toward Caesarea. And in Caesarea, Peter does not lose his nerve and sink beneath the waves but rises to the occasion. The book of Acts reports that Peter "fairly exploded with his

177

good news," announcing: "It's God's own truth, nothing could be plainer: God plays no favorites! It makes no difference who you are or where you're from—if you want God and are ready to do as [God] says, the door is open. The Message [God] sent to the children of Israel—that through Jesus Christ everything is being put together again—well, [God's] doing it everywhere, among everyone" (Acts 10:34-36 *The Message*). That day the Holy Spirit is said to have come over Cornelius's whole household, moving Peter to baptize them all into full faith and fellowship in the Christian community, forever altering the course of Christianity.

Yet there was still one more great challenge before Peter. If the Christian community was to open the door wide to Gentiles, others would need to be as convinced as Peter that what he did in Caesarea was in accordance with God's will. Most were skeptical. Before long, Peter was called before the high council in Jerusalem to account for his actions. The pressure was on!

It is one thing to make a private decision about what God is up to in the world and act on it yourself. It is quite another to stand before a group of the Christian community's most trusted and respected leaders—most of whom think you have committed apostasy, flaunting both Scripture and tradition—and argue that the Spirit is calling the community to open the doors wide to those they have previously excluded. Would Peter lose his nerve?

Here again, one of Peter's great failures became a source of strength. Peter knew what it was like to know the truth yet deny it before others. Years earlier, when Jesus forewarned his disciples of his coming arrest and execution, Peter insisted, "Lord, I am ready to go with you to prison and to death!" Jesus responded, "I tell you, Peter, the cock will not crow this day, until you have denied three times that you know me" (Luke 24:33-34 NRSV). Sure enough, when questioned three separate times about his relationship with Jesus outside the high priest's house where Jesus was being held after his arrest, Peter categorically denied that he knew Jesus all three times. The sound of the cock crowing must have fallen on Peter's ears like a sledgehammer, filling him with grief and crushing any hope of ever becoming the Rock upon which Jesus would build his community.

Standing before the high council in Jerusalem to answer for his actions, Peter's threefold denial cannot have been far from his mind. The pressure to conform and either deny his actions or call them a mistake must have been enormous. Yet this time, there was absolutely no way he was going to let fear get the better of him. Peter knew what it was like to live with bitter regret over failing to bear witness to what his heart knew to be true. He wasn't going to relive the experience. Peter would follow the Spirit's call no matter how deeply it broke with his tradition or the storm of controversy that would surely erupt over his testimony.

In response to the red-faced council of church leaders, Peter spoke confidently regarding his Gentile converts: "If God gave them the same gift [of the Holy Spirit] he gave us who believed in the Lord Jesus Christ, then who am I? Could I stand in God's way?" (Acts 11:17).

Through Peter's testimony, he not only walked upon the stormy sea without sinking, he *crossed* it. While it would be decades before the Christian church would fully accept Gentiles into their community, the door opened for the first time here at this council. Enough leaders were persuaded (probably thunderstruck!) that day that they gave Peter their blessing to continue reaching out to those who had been so thoroughly excluded.

Through Peter's experience in Joppa, Caesarea, and before the Jerusalem council, perhaps he came to realize for the first time what Jesus intended when he announced to the disciples that his church would be founded upon a *sinking* Rock. It is a Rock that cannot stand alone upon the water, but can only be held up by a power much greater than itself; a Rock upon which all failure no matter how bitter may ultimately be redeemed and all fear is swallowed by the sea. A church built upon this Rock is not the church of the perfect, but the church of the misfits. Its saints find their place in this world in the heart of their struggles, not merely in their absence. This is a church born in the Dark Wood. It is a community that continues to thrive there, continuing to learn what it means to welcome and embrace those who have been excluded.

Whether or not you consider yourself a follower of Jesus, perhaps within the Dark Wood of your own experience you will find the blessing of Jesus through the companionship of Peter. You will not likely find Peter walking beside you simply when you *believe* the right way, or *act* the right way, but when you *fail*. Perhaps you will find Peter offering a few suggestions about how to fail *in just the right way*.

My hope is that you will also experience the voice of the Spirit speaking within your struggles—as I did while floating in the waters of Easedale Tarn: *You have a place in this world; a place where everything comes together in your body and you disappear into a seamless whole. Get over your fat little belly* [or whatever shortcomings afflict you] *and inhabit this world with your fullest self.*

As you make your way through the Dark Wood, inhabiting this world with your fullest self, I leave you with this prayerful blessing, a version of which I offer to my congregation every Sunday:

May the Spirit of the Living God,
Made known to us most fully within life's Dark Wood:
Go before you to show you the way;
Go above you to watch over you;
Go behind you to push you into places you may not
necessarily go yourself;
Go beneath you to uphold and uplift you;
Go beside you to be your strong and constant companion;
And dwell within you to remind you that you are surely not
alone,
And that you are loved—loved beyond your wildest
imagination.
And may the fire of God's blessing burn brightly
Upon you, and within you,
Now and always.
Amen.

THE PHOENIX
AFFIRMATIONS

Christian love of God includes:[1]

1. Walking fully in the path of Jesus, without denying the legitimacy of other paths that God may provide for humanity;

2. Listening for God's Word which comes through daily prayer and meditation, studying the ancient testimonies which we call Scripture, and attending to God's present activity in the world;

3. Celebrating the God whose Spirit pervades and whose glory is reflected in all of God's Creation, including the earth and its ecosystems, the sacred and secular, the Christian and non-Christian, the human and non-human;

4. Expressing our love in worship that is as sincere, vibrant, and artful as it is scriptural.

Christian love of neighbor includes:

5. Engaging people authentically, as Jesus did, treating all as creations made in God's very image, regardless of race, gender,

sexual orientation, age, physical or mental ability, nationality, or economic class;

6. Standing, as Jesus does, with the outcast and oppressed, the denigrated and afflicted, seeking peace and justice with or without the support of others;

7. Preserving religious freedom and the church's ability to speak prophetically to government by resisting the commingling of church and state;

8. Walking humbly with God, acknowledging our own shortcomings while honestly seeking to understand and call forth the best in others, including those who consider us their enemies;

Christian love of self includes:

9. Basing our lives on the faith that in Christ all things are made new and that we, and all people, are loved beyond our wildest imagination—for eternity;

10. Claiming the sacredness of both our minds and our hearts, and recognizing that faith and science, doubt and belief serve the pursuit of truth;

11. Caring for our bodies and insisting on taking time to enjoy the benefits of prayer, reflection, worship, and recreation in addition to work;

12. Acting on the faith that we are born with a meaning and purpose; a vocation and ministry that serve to strengthen and extend God's realm of love.

NOTES

1. WHERE WE FIND OURSELVES

1. Dante Alighieri, *La Divina Commedia*, Inferno: Canto I. Author's translation.

2. Michael Casey, *Toward God: The Ancient Wisdom of Western Prayer* (Liguori, MO: Liguori/Triumph, 1996), 24.

3. Saint Augustine, *Confessions*, i.1.

4. Jack Levison, promo video for *Fresh Air*, www.youtube.com /watch?v=Sld7qMzQ918.

5. Thomas Merton, *Day of a Stranger* (Layton, UT: Gibbs M. Smith, 1981), 41.

6. This phrase, which Jung found in the Latin writings of Desiderius Erasmus, was inscribed in Latin above the doorway of Jung's house and upon his tomb, "*Vocatus atque non vocatus, Deus aderit.*"

2. THE GIFT OF UNCERTAINTY

1. John Ortberg, *Faith and Doubt* (Grand Rapids, MI: Zondervan, 2008), 137.

2. David Whyte, *Crossing the Unknown Sea* (New York: Riverhead Books, 2001), 129–35.

3. THE GIFT OF EMPTINESS

1. Coleman Barks, trans., *The Essential Rumi, New Expanded Edition* (San Francisco: Harper One, 2004), 36.

2. Forrest Church, *Lifecraft* (Boston: Beacon, 2001), xi–xii.

3. "Penn Researchers Calculate How Much the Eye Tells the Brain," The University of Pennsylvania School of Medicine, July 26, 2006, www.uphs.upenn.edu/news/News_Releases/jul06/retinput.htm.

4. See the information for Los Angeles County, California, from the United States Census Bureau, http://quickfacts.census.gov/qfd /states/06/06037.html.

5. Parker Palmer, *A Hidden Wholeness: The Journey Toward an Undivided Life* (San Francisco: Jossey-Bass, 2004), 58–59.

4. THE GIFT OF BEING THUNDERSTRUCK

1. Susan Orlean (book, *The Orchid Thief*), Charlie Kaufman and Donald Kaufman (screenplay), *Adaptation* (Los Angeles: Columbia/Tristar, 2002).

2. Phyllis Tickle addresses this question in a *Darkwood Brew* program entitled, "The Great Convergence, Episode 5: Was It the Holy Spirit or Just the Pizza?" See http://darkwoodbrew.org/the-great-conver gence-e5/.

5. THE GIFT OF GETTING LOST

1. David Wagoner, "Lost," *Traveling Light: Collected and New Poems* (Champaign: University of Illinois Press, 1999), 10.

2. Steve Koren, Mark O'Keefe, Steve Oedekerk, *Bruce Almighty* (Los Angeles: Universal Pictures, 2003).

3. William Blake, *Milton, A Poem* (London: Tate Gallery Publications, 1993), plate 35, line 42.

4. Anne Lamott, *Bird by Bird* (New York: Anchor Books, 1994), 18.

6. THE GIFT OF TEMPTATION

1. William Blake, *Milton, A Poem* (London: Tate Gallery Publications, 1993), plate 35, line 42.

7. THE GIFT OF DISAPPEARING

1. David Whyte, "Tobar Phadraic," *River Flow: New and Selected Poems* (Langley, WA: Many Rivers, 2007), 287.

8. THE GIFT OF MISFITS

1. The verb commonly translated as "come near" may also be rendered as a completed action, as in "now here." The word translated as "repent" literally means to "change your way of thinking."

2. Bhikkhu Bodhi, "The Collected Discourses of the Buddha: A New Translation of the Samyutta Nikaya" (Somerville: Wisdom Publications, Sakkasamyutta, Dhajjaggasutta [3], 2000), 319–21.

3. You can find and participate in this community on the web at www.darkwoodbrew.org.

4. Brian McLaren, *A Generous Orthodoxy* (Grand Rapids: Zondervan, 2004).

5. Deep in the heartland of America, these values are given concrete expression through Omaha, Nebraska's Tri-Faith Initiative. On the thirty-five-acre Tri-Faith campus, Jewish, Christian, and Muslim faith communities are building separate worship facilities and a shared community center for fellowship and education in the geographic center of Omaha. My church, Countryside Community Church, is the Christian partner in this endeavor. The intention of each of the Tri-Faith partners is neither to merge the three Abrahamic faiths into a new one nor to share a relationship built upon the lowest common denominator. Rather, we are finding the exploration of our differences to be as fruitful and inspiring to faith as discovering the increasing common ground we share. Together, we are learning what it means for "COEXIST" to be more than a bumper sticker. Find more at www.trifaith.org.

9. WHERE WE GO FROM HERE

1. J. Brian Tucker, "God-Fearers: Literary Foil or Historical Reality in the Book of Acts?" *Journal of Biblical Studies* 4, no. 1 (2005): 21–39.

APPENDIX: THE PHOENIX AFFIRMATIONS

1. Eric Elnes, The Phoenix Affirmations, September 3, 2010, https://phoenixaffirmations.wordpress.com/. For even more information on the Phoenix Affirmations, see my book *The Phoenix Affirmations: A New Vision for the Future of Christianity* (San Francisco: Jossy-Bass, 2006).

Eric Elnes (PhD, Princeton Theological Seminary) is a pastor, speaker, and media host. He is the author of *The Phoenix Affirmations: A New Vision for the Future of Christianity* and *Igniting Worship: The Seven Deadly Sins*. His book *Asphalt Jesus: Finding a New Christian Faith on the Highways of America* was the result of his 2,500-mile walk from Phoenix to Washington, DC, which promoted awareness of progressive / emerging Christian faith and inspired a feature-length film called *The Asphalt Gospel*. Since then, his interactive weekly webcast "Darkwood Brew" has gathered people from around the world for an engaging exploration of Convergence Christianity. Elnes lives with his wife and daughters in Omaha, Nebraska, where he also serves as senior pastor of Countryside Community Church (UCC).

Find out more at GiftsOfTheDarkWood.com
and DarkwoodBrew.com